Language Technology and Resources for a Fair, Inclusive, and Safe Society (LATERAISSE 2022)

AA004810

Held at LREC 2022

Marseille, France
20 – 25 June 2022

Editors:

Kolawole Adebayo
Rohan Nanda
Kanishk Verma
Brian Davis

ISBN: 978-1-7138-6124-9

Printed from e-media with permission by:

Curran Associates, Inc.
57 Morehouse Lane
Red Hook, NY 12571

Some format issues inherent in the e-media version may also appear in this print version.

Copyright© (2022) by the Association for Computational Linguistics
All rights reserved.
Copyright for individual papers remains with the authors and are licensed under a Creative Commons 4.0 license, CC-BY-ND. (https://creativecommons.org/licenses/by-nd/4.0/)

Printed with permission by Curran Associates, Inc. (2022)

For permission requests, please contact the Association for Computational Linguistics at the address below.

Association for Computational Linguistics
209 N. Eighth Street
Stroudsburg, Pennsylvania 18360

Phone: 1-570-476-8006
Fax: 1-570-476-0860

acl@aclweb.org

Additional copies of this publication are available from:

Curran Associates, Inc.
57 Morehouse Lane
Red Hook, NY 12571 USA
Phone: 845-758-0400
Fax: 845-758-2633
Email: curran@proceedings.com
Web: www.proceedings.com

LREC 2022 Workshop
Language Resources and Evaluation Conference
20-25 June 2022

Language Technology and Resources for a Fair, Inclusive, and Safe Society (LATERAISSE)

PROCEEDINGS

Editors:
Kolawole Adebayo
Rohan Nanda
Kanishk Verma
Brian Davis

Proceedings of the LREC 2022 workshop on Language Technology and Resources for a Fair, Inclusive, and Safe Society (LATERAISSE 2022)

Edited by:
Kolawole Adebayo
Rohan Nanda
Kanishk Verma
Brian Davis

For more information:
European Language Resources Association (ELRA)
9 rue des Cordelières
75013, Paris
France
http://www.elra.info
Email: lrec@elda.org

© European Language Resources Association (ELRA)

These workshop proceedings are licensed under a Creative Commons
Attribution-NonCommercial 4.0 International License

Preface

This volume documents the proceedings of the First Workshop on Language Technology and Resources for a Fair, Inclusive, and Safe Society (LateRAISSE), a full-day workshop held on June 25, 2022, as part of the LREC 2022 conference (International Conference on Language Resources and Evaluation). The workshop aims to bring together researchers and scholars working on the creation and use of language resources and tools for identifying and raising awareness of bias and discrimination in social computational systems and also with a focus on hate, harassment, and bullying in online spaces. In addition, the workshop encouraged the participation of technical and non-technical experts in the computing and social science sub-disciplines to focus on the issue of social inclusion and safety from different perspectives. We solicited research work that implements relevant state-of-the-art machine learning and natural language processing technologies for a fair, inclusive and safe society, through the development of unbiased and inclusive language tools and resources in three main fields - Human Resources; Law; and Online Hate and Harassment. We particularly encouraged submissions based on low resource languages.

We received eight full paper submissions to the workshop. Each paper was assigned to two technical reviewers (with a Computer Science background) and one researcher with a Social Science background considering the reviewer's expertise and the domain of the papers. Four papers were unconditionally accepted after a qualitative blind review process; two were conditionally accepted, while two were rejected.
Out of the six accepted papers, three papers address the issues of gender and racial bias in the society with NLP through the analysis of word embeddings and multilingual corpus. Equally, two papers presented their studies on cyber-bullying and hate speech identification using NLP and Machine learning while the remaining paper bonds with the legal theme of the workshop. The accepted papers in the proceedings have been carefully selected to reflect the aims and objectives of the workshop.

In terms of the geographical diversity of the authors, we received submissions from India, the Netherlands, France, Bangladesh, Turkey, and Ireland. The overall acceptance rate for the workshop was 75%. However, the number of papers submitted as well as the spread of the workshop's research themes may have contributed to the high acceptance rate.

We hope that readers will find the papers interesting and that they continue to provoke intellectual engagement around the research themes of the workshop.

Sincerely,

Dr. Kolawole Adebayo - ADAPT Centre - Dublin City University, Ireland
Dr. Rohan Nanda - Institute of Data Science (IDS) and Maastricht Law and Tech Lab - Maastricht University, Netherlands
Kanishk Verma - ADAPT Centre, DCU Anti Bullying Centre - Dublin City University, Ireland
Prof. Brian Davis - ADAPT Centre - Dublin City University, Ireland

Organizers

Kolawole Adebayo – ADAPT Centre – Dublin City University, Ireland
Rohan Nanda – Institute of Data Science (IDS) and Maastricht Law and Tech Lab –Maastricht University, Netherlands
Kanishk Verma – ADAPT Centre, DCU Anti Bullying Centre – Dublin City University, Ireland
Brian Davis – ADAPT Centre – Dublin City University, Ireland

Program Committee:

Prof. Guido Boella (University of Turin, Italy)
Prof. Laurette Pretorious (University of South Africa)
Prof. Amaya Nogales Gomez (Universite Cote D'Azur, Inria, France)
Prof. Luigi Di Caro (University of Turin, Italy)
Prof. Alexandra Klimova (ITMO University, Russia)
Prof. Jennifer Foster (Dublin City University, Ireland)
Dr. Maja Popovic (Dublin City University)
Dr. Joachim Wagner (Dublin City University, Ireland)
Dr. Jerry Spanakis (University of Maastricht, Netherland)
Dr. Livio Robaldo (Swansea University, UK)
Dr. Giovanni Siragusa (University of Turin, Italy)
Dr. Cristiana Santos (Utrecht University, Netherlands)
Dr. Tijana Milosevic (Dublin City University, Ireland)
Dr. Emilio Sulis (University of Turin, Italy)
Dr. Alunge Rogers (European Data Protection Office, Brussels, Belgium)
Dr. Robert Muthuri (Strathmore University)
Dr. John Roberto (ADAPT Centre, Ireland)
Dr. Reka Markovich (University of Luxembourg)
Dr. Eduard Fosch Villaronga (Leiden University, Netherlands)
Dr. Nishtha Jain (ADAPT Centre, Ireland)
Senthil Kumar B (SSN College of Engineering, India)

Table of Contents

Conference Program

Proceedings of LATERAISSE Workshop @LREC2022, pages 1–7
Marseille, 25 June 2022
© European Language Resources Association (ELRA), licensed under CC-BY-NC-4.0

Casteism in India, But not Racism - A Study of Bias in Word Embeddings of Indian Languages

Senthil Kumar B[1], Pranav Tiwari[2], Aman Chandra Kumar[2], Aravindan Chandrabose[1]
[1]Sri Sivasubramaniya Nadar College of Engineering, Chennai, India
[2]Indian Institute of Information Technology, Tiruchirappalli, India
{senthil, aravindanc}@ssn.edu.in
{pranavtiwari548, amanchandrakumar202}@gmail.com

Abstract

In this paper, we studied the gender bias in monolingual word embeddings of two Indian languages Hindi and Tamil. Tamil is one of the classical languages of India from the Dravidian language family. In Indian society and culture, instead of racism, a similar type of discrimination called *casteism* is against the subgroup of peoples representing lower class or *Dalits*. The word embeddings measurement to evaluate bias using the WEAT score reveals that the embeddings are biased with gender and casteism which is in line with the common stereotypical human biases.

Keywords: bias in word embeddings, gender bias, caste bias, WEAT, Indian languages

1. Introduction

A language is a wonderful tool for communication. It has powered the human race for centuries and continues to be at the heart of our culture. India has more than 270 languages or dialects spoken as its mother tongue. Of 121 languages that are spoken by 10,000 or more people, 22 languages comprising 123 mother tongues are specified in the Eighth Schedule to the Constitution of India as Scheduled Languages. [1]. Hindi and Tamil are the Scheduled languages of India.

Based on cultural linkages and unfavorable social biases, NLP models are trained with a variety of biases and discrimination. Word embeddings have become a standard resource for representing the text in ML-based NLP applications. Generating a good word embedding is very important to avoid bias in the downstream tasks. Learning a high-quality word representation is extremely important for various syntactic and semantic tasks. The methods to evaluate the quality of word embeddings are categorized into intrinsic and extrinsic methods. Extrinsic methods use word embeddings as input features to a downstream task and measure changes in performance metrics specific to that task. But the intrinsic evaluation methods test the quality of an embedding independent of a specific NLP task. One technique to measure the quality of word embedding is to check whether it is unbiased towards gender, racism, religion, demographic, etc., using bias evaluation metrics like WEAT.

Despite the diversity, bias in word embeddings of Indian languages is studied less. So far, bias is experimented with Hindi, Bengali and Telugu languages of India. Hindi and Bengali are the languages of the Indo-Aryan (or Indic language) family. Tamil and Telugu are the languages of thfe Dravidian family and Tamil is a classical Dravidian language. Our study shows bias in the Tamil language which is highly agglutinate and also in Hindi. Instead of *racism*, we experiment with a type of bias called *casteism* which is highly prevalent in Indian culture. Caste systems in India have its root in medieval, early-modern, and modern India (Bayly, 2001).

The rest of the paper is structured as follows. Section 2 describes related works on these problems and provides context on why the problem is difficult and important to solve. Next, in sections 3, we describe the datasets and bias measure which are used to measure it. In Section 4 we analyse and present the results and conclusion about our work in section 5.

2. Related Work

Gender bias appears to be a common stereotype that exists across vast majority of data resources. An illustrious work by Bolukbasi et al. (2016) observed gender bias in Word2Vec word embeddings. They showed that gender bias could be found by identifying the direction in embedding subspace and could be neutralized. Caliskan et al. (2017) measured the bias in the Word2Vec embeddings on Google News corpus and pre-trained GloVe using WEAT, WEFAT score. Escudé Font et al. (2019) found gender bias in the translation of English-Spanish in the news domain. Embeddings

[1]Census of India, 2021

of gendered languages such as Spanish and French contain gender bias. Zhou et al. (2019) observed the bias in bilingual embeddings from MUSE while translating ES-EN and FR-EN, where both the Spanish and French are gendered languages. To neutralize gender in word embeddings, GN-GloVe (Zhao et al., 2018) is used to mitigate gender bias in word representations. Apart from gender bias, Manzini et al. (2019) found ethnicity and religion bias by extending WEAT to measure the bias over a Word2Vec model. Research on race in NLP remains less and ignored in many NLP tasks. Field et al. (2021) survey on racism in NLP research shows that only 13 papers from ACL anthology focus on racial bias in text representations (LMs, embeddings). The survey highlighted that the NLP research fails to account for the multidimensional race. Hasanuzzaman et al. (2017) shows that racism is in link with location information instead of gender. Bansal et al. (2021) measured gender bias using intrinsic, extrinsic bias and debias the word embeddings for three Indian languages (Hindi, Bengali, Telugu) in addition to English.
The challenges in Indian languages are:
1. The semantics of gender words may vary from one language to another.
2. While Bolukbasi et al. (2016) leverages the pronouns (e.g.,she/he) to construct gendered directions this might not be possible for many languages (e.g., In Tamil, the same pronoun அவர் is used to refer to both the male and female genders).
3. Certain terms in Tamil have male honorific forms, do not have the corresponding female honorific forms. One may be tempted to say the forms listed as masculine honorific forms are neutral forms. Yet, in actual use, these often assume male reference.

Male	Female	Honorific	English
பாடகன்	பாடகி	பாடகர்	singer
தலைவன்	தலைவி	தலைவர்	leader

Table 1: Gender-neutral or honorific terms in Tamil

2.1. Why Casteism but not Racism?

In gender classification based on photographs of faces, Buolamwini and Gebru (2018) could draw the connection between phenotype and race. They noted that racial categories are unstable and that phenotype can vary widely within a racial or ethnic category. Moreover Benthall and Haynes (2019) claims that the acquisition of a race by a person depends on several different factors, including bio-metric properties, socioeconomic class, and ancestral geographic and national origin. Hence Hanna et al. (2020; Benthall and Haynes (2019; Field et al. (2021) argue that race is a multi-dimensional and can refer to a variety of different perspectives. During the World Conference against Racism (WCAR) by United Nations in 2001, which discussed various manifestations of racism, the position of the Indian government was that the caste is not a race and hence is not relevant at conference (Pinto, 2001). Due to its multi-dimensional nature, no widely accepted categorization scheme and the Indian government stance, casteism is varied from racism.
Our contributions include considering two Indian languages, each from the Indo-Aryan and Dravidian families, and bias analysis concerning gender and casteism. As per the literature survey and to our knowledge, this is the first report on 1) bias in Tamil language embeddings, 2) the discrimination of subgroup of people in India under "casteism" is reflected in word embeddings. The choice of the current set of languages is motivated by the knowledge of the authors in these languages.

3. Experiment

Neural network models are quite powerful and efficient, but at the same time, these models inherently contain problematic biases in many forms. Many pre-trained language models such as Word2Vec, GloVe, ELMo, fastText, etc., are widely available for developers to generate word embeddings, but they should also be aware of what biases they contain and how they might exacerbate in those applications. In our experiment, two pre-trained language models: Word2Vec (Hindi) and fastText (Hindi and Tamil) are used to obtain the word embeddings. To check whether the embeddings of these models are biased or not, the WEAT metric is used to find its association or bias which is in line with the human bias.

3.1. Datasets

For gender bias, most of the words are taken from Caliskan et al. (2017) study on gender-biased words using male vs female and career vs family. The male vs female words is also measured against the male vs female traits (or adjectives). In Indian languages, some of the words are used in their transliterated form instead of their equivalent linguistic form. For example, the words उप-चारिका (Nurse) is less frequently used instead of its transliterated form नर्स. The frequently used form is included in this study. Table 2 lists the statistics of the dataset for the Hindi and Tamil languages. Words such as loyal, family, happy, abuse, murder, assault and jail are taken from pleasant vs. unpleasant words of Caliskan et al. (2017). The other words are considered in the context of cultural and societal practices followed by the Indian people.

Targets	Hindi	Tamil	Attributes	Hindi	Tamil
Career vs Family	4	5	Male vs Female	10	7
Male vs. Female Traits	5	5	Male vs Female	10	11
Pleasant vs Unpleasant	18	8	Upper vs Lower	6	6
High-paid vs Low-paid	10	16	Upper vs Lower	6	6

Table 2: The number of words used in the target and attribute sets for Hindi and Tamil languages.

Gathering data to examine a new bias type called casteism in NLP is challenging. There is no exact translation of *caste* in Indian languages, but *varna* and *jati* are the two most approximate terms. The caste emanates from four *varnas* or *jati* system in Indian culture. For bias in casteism, the words are inferred from the four *varnas* system in India. The castes under four *varnas* or *jati* are grouped into a single, the remaining are considered as others or *untouchables* or Scheduled Castes, the official term as per the Constitution of India [2]. We label the group of four as upper and the other as lower caste. The peoples of upper caste are majority than the lower caste and hence lower caste is also referred to as minorities. The set of attribute words for caste in Hindi and Tamil is shown in Table 3 for upper caste and Table 4 for lower caste. '-' in the table indicates that a particular caste word is infrequently used in context in spite of its prevalence.

Hindi	Tamil	English
ब्राह्मण	பிராமணர்கள்	brahmins
क्षत्रिय	க்ஷத்திரியர்கள்	kshatriyas
वैश्य	வைசியர்கள்	vaisyas
-	சூத்திரர்கள்	kshudras
उच्च	உயர்	upper
पंडित	-	priest

Table 3: Hindi/Tamil upper caste words

Hindi	Tamil	English
हरिजन	ஹரிஜனங்கள்	harijans
दलितों	தலித்	dalits
अनुसूचित	அட்டவணைப்படுத்தப்பட்ட	schedule caste
अछूतों	தீண்டத்தகாதவர்கள்	untouchables
निचली	கீழ்	lower

Table 4: Hindi/Tamil lower caste words

3.2. Word2Vec model

Word2Vec [3] model trained on Hindi CoNLL 17 corpus using Continous Skipgram model in dimension 100.

3.3. fastText model

The fastText [4] is a pre-trained language model trained on Wikipedia and the Common Crawl to represent word vectors for different 157 languages. Each of these models was trained on Wikipedia dumps of the respective languages using CBOW with position-weights, in dimension 300, with character n-grams of length 5. It was observed that for languages with small Wikipedia, such as Finnish or Hindi, using the crawl data leads to great improvement in performance. However for the low resource languages such as Hindi, the quality of the obtained word vectors is much lower than for other languages (Grave et al., 2018).

3.4. Correlation with Human Biases using WEAT

We used the metric **Word Embedding Association Test (WEAT)** proposed by Caliskan et al. (2017) which uses permutation testing to demonstrate and quantify bias. WEAT measures the similarity of words by using the cosine between the pair of vectors of those words. It was applied to GloVe and Word2Vec vectors. WEAT can also be applied to other models. Consider the two sets of target words (like politician, engineer, tailor, ... and nanny, nurse, librarian, ...) and two sets of attribute words (like man, boy, ... and woman, girl ...) to measure the bias against the social attributes and roles. In mathematical terms, X and Y are assumed to be sets of target words of equal size, and A,B are the two sets of attribute words. The permutation test over X and Y is,

$$s(X,Y,A,B) = \sum_{x \in X} s(x,A,B) - \sum_{y \in Y} s(y,A,B)$$

The degree of bias for each target concept is calculated as,

$$s(w,A,B) = mean_{a \in A} cos(\vec{w}, \vec{a}) - mean_{b \in B} cos(\vec{w}, \vec{b})$$

where $cos(\vec{a}, \vec{b})$ is the cosine similarity between the two vector embeddings. In other words, s(w,A,B) measures the association of the word w with the attribute, and s(X,Y,A,B) measures the

[2]Caste System in India
[3]NLPL word embedding repository
[4]fastText for different 157 languages

differential association of the two sets of target words with the attribute. The degree d to which the model associates the sets of target words with the sets of attribute words is,

$$d = \frac{mean_{x \in X} s(x, A, B) - mean_{y \in Y} s(y, A, B)}{std - dev_{w \in X \sqcup Y} s(w, A, B)}$$

For example, consider the target lists for the WEAT test are pleasant and unpleasant words, and the attributes are caste discrimination in India such as upper caste (e.g., "brahmins", "vaisyas", "kshatriyas") and lower caste (e.g., "dalits", "harijans", "untouchables"). The overall test score is the degree to which pleasant words are more associated with the upper caste, relative to lower caste. A high positive score means that pleasant words are more related to upper caste, and a high negative score means that unpleasant words are more associated with upper caste.

4. Result Analysis

Word2Vec (Skipgram) embeddings are used for Hindi language only. The fastText embeddings of Hindi and Tamil languages are measured for bias. We consider the following two target sets:
1) career vs. family, sentiment words or traits of male vs. female.
2) pleasant vs. unpleasant, career of upper vs. lower caste.
For the above target sets, the corresponding attribute sets are 1)male vs. female and 2)upper vs. lower caste. Note that from tables 5-12, the words are arranged in descending order of bias score. For example, occupation (career vs family) words are sorted with the degree of bias in descending order for Hindi in Table 5.

Male	Female
सेनाध्यक (commander)	बाई (maid)
सैनिक (soldier)	दाई (babysitter)
राजनीतिज्ञ (politician)	नर्स (nurse)
शिकारी (hunter)	रसोइया (cook)

Table 5: Hindi Male/Female-biased words for Occupation using fastText

For Tamil, the occupations of gender (career vs. family) differs from Hindi, because of the demographic or regional cultural influence. In both the languages, occupational words like politician, hunter and nurse, maid are biased towards male and female respectively.
The male vs female traits (adjectives) are different across the demography irrespective of gender as shown in Table 7 and 8. For example high degree of male trait word exercise (உடற்பயிற்சி) in Tamil

Male	Female
வேட்டைக்காரன் (hunter)	பணிப்பெண் (maid)
அரசியல்வாதி (politician)	செவிலியர் (nurse)
பொறியாளர் (engineer)	ஒப்பனையாளர் (stylist)
காவல் (police)	நடனக்கலைஞர் (dancer)
சிப்பாய் (soldier)	கைவினை (craft person)

Table 6: Tamil Male/Female-biased words for Occupation using fastText

is not the same in Hindi. For Hindi, it is combat (मुकाबला).

Male	Female
मुकाबला (combat)	सुंदरता (beauty)
अभ्यास (practice)	तलाक (divorce)
हमला (attack)	शादी (wedding)
घायल (injured)	परिपक्व (mature)
परिश्रम (hardwork)	प्यार (love)

Table 7: Hindi Male vs Female Traits (adjectives) using fastText

In both the languages, sentiment words like combat/battle, attack are associated towards male and beauty, wedding, divorce are associated towards female.

Male	Female
உடற்பயிற்சி (exercise)	விவாகரத்து(divorce)
இரக்கமற்ற (ruthless)	அழகு (beauty)
சக்தி (power)	நகை (jewel)
போர் (battle)	திருமணம்(wedding)
தாக்குதல் (attack)	நளினம் (elegance)

Table 8: Tamil Male vs Female Traits (adjectives) using fastText

4.1. Caste Bias in Indian Languages

Castes are rigid social groups characterized by hereditary transmission of lifestyle, occupation, and social status. This is ingrained in the social and economic status of peoples across castes in Indian culture. We measured the bias against the caste words for the two attribute sets: 1)Pleasant vs. unpleasant words and 2)Career words (high-paid vs low-paid). Some of the adjective words are used to denote a particular group of caste. Those words are categorized into pleasant and unpleasant words. The careers of the minority group or lower caste also differs from that of the upper caste group.

upper	lower
वैदिक (vaidic)	हमला (assault)
धनी (rich)	दुर्व्यवहार (abuse)
ज्ञान (knowledge)	जेल (jail)
भाग्यशाली (fortunate)	हत्या (murder)
निष्ठावान (loyal)	श्रम (labour)
साहित्य (literature)	निरक्षर (illiterate)
परिवार (family)	उत्पीड़ित (oppressed)
खुश (happy)	घृणा (hatred)
शक्ति (strength)	सताया (persecuted)

Table 9: Hindi Caste-biased Pleasant vs. unpleasant words using fastText

From the Table 9-10, the bias in the embeddings clearly shows the discrimination of the lower caste minority in India. India after 1947, enacted many affirmative action policies for the upliftment of historically marginalized groups. These policies included reserving a quota of places for these groups in higher education and government employment. But still, the word embeddings reflects the caste stereotypes that still exists in the Indian society. In Table 11-12, the bias in the embeddings clearly reflects the discrimination in the social-economic structure of the lower caste minority in India. The occupations of Dalits vary from caste to caste and geographical area. Most of them work with human waste, leather, dead bodies, etc., (Kaminsky; Long, 2011).

upper	lower
வேத (vedic)	தாழ்த்தப்பட்ட (downtrodden)
அறிவாளி (knowledge)	ஒடுக்கப்பட்ட (oppressed)
அதிர்ஷ்டசாலி(fortunate)	அடிமைப்படுத்தப்பட்ட (enslaved)
கல்வி (education)	தாக்குதல் (attack)
சக்தி (power)	சிறை (jail)
கற்றவர் (literate)	கொலை (murder)

Table 10: Tamil Caste-biased Pleasant vs. unpleasant words using fastText

Table-13 shows the WEAT scores for the different embedding models for the four different target and attribute sets. The score indicates that the direction of measured bias is in line with the common human biases. For the upper vs lower and career dataset, the negative WEAT score for the Word2Vec Hindi embeddings implies that the bias is against the common human biases. Generally, Hindi language embeddings are less biased than Tamil towards careers of upper and lower caste peoples. To prove that racism is not much prevalent in India, a set of racial prejudice words *chink, chinky, chinese, nepali* against the north-east Indians (Haokip, 2021) are paired with the pleasant vs. unpleasant words in Hindi. The negative score indicates that the embeddings are racial-free.

upper	lower
योद्धा (warrior)	मजदूरी (wage)
अफ़सर (officer)	बेरोजगार (unemployed)
अभियंता (engineer)	कुम्हार *(potter)*
शिक्षक (teacher)	किसान *(farmer)*
वैज्ञानिक (scientist)	रक्षक *(protector)*
संगीत (music)	मोची *(cobbler)*
अनुसंधान (research)	चौकीदार *(watchman)*

Table 11: Hindi Caste-biased career words using fastText. Italicised is unbiased.

upper	lower
போர்வீரன் (warrior)	கல்லறைத்தொழிலாளி (cemetry worker)
வணிகர் (merchant)	தொழிலாளி (labour)
விஞ்ஞானி (scientist)	துப்புரவாளர் (sweeper)
பொறியாளர் (engineer)	செருப்புத்தொழிலாளி (cobbler)
அதிகாரி (officer)	காவலாளி (watchman)
ஆசிரியர் (teacher)	விவசாயி (farmer)

Table 12: Tamil Caste-biased career words using fastText

5. Conclusion

In this paper, instead of racism which is not applicable to India, casteism as per the the Indian social system is included in word embedding bias evaluation. We have identified the sets of caste words in Hindi and Tamil languages for caste bias analysis. WEAT metric is used to evaluate the word embeddings for gender and caste bias. The bias study on monolingual word embeddings of Word2Vec and fastText for two of the Indian languages such as Hindi and Tamil reveals that the gender and caste bias prevails in line with the stereotypes. From the literature and to our knowledge this is the first paper that reports the bias in Tamil word embeddings and caste bias in word embeddings of Indian languages. Also proved that the embeddings are racial-free.

In future, we will extend the bias analysis by including more Indian languages and apply debiasing techniques to mitigate the bias in Indian language word embeddings.

6. Bibliographical References

Bansal, S., Garimella, V., Suhane, A., and Mukherjee, A. (2021). Debiasing multilingual

Targets	Attributes	Word2Vec(H)	fastText(H)	fastText(T)
Career vs Family	Male vs Female	1.15	1.85	1.07
Male vs. Female Traits	Male vs Female	1.58	1.79	0.89
Pleasant vs Unpleasant	Upper vs Lower	1.08	1.52	1.84
High-paid vs Low-paid	Upper vs Lower	-0.38	0.99	1.55
Indian vs North-east	Pleasant vs Unpleasant	-	-0.36	-

Table 13: WEAT scores for different embedding models. Negative value indicates that the direction of the measured bias is against the common human biases. H-Hindi, T-Tamil

word embeddings: A case study of three indian languages. In *Proceedings of the 32nd ACM Conference on Hypertext and Social Media*, HT '21, page 27–34, New York, NY, USA. Association for Computing Machinery.

Bayly, S. (2001). Cambridge University Press. ISBN 978-0-521-26434-1.

Benthall, S. and Haynes, B. D. (2019). Racial categories in machine learning. In *Proceedings of the Conference on Fairness, Accountability, and Transparency*, FAT* '19, page 289–298, New York, NY, USA. Association for Computing Machinery.

Bolukbasi, T., Chang, K.-W., Zou, J., Saligrama, V., and Kalai, A. (2016). Man is to computer programmer as woman is to homemaker? debiasing word embeddings. In *Proceedings of the 30th International Conference on Neural Information Processing Systems*, NIPS'16, page 4356–4364, Red Hook, NY, USA. Curran Associates Inc.

Buolamwini, J. and Gebru, T. (2018). Gender shades: Intersectional accuracy disparities in commercial gender classification. In Sorelle A. Friedler et al., editors, *Proceedings of the 1st Conference on Fairness, Accountability and Transparency*, volume 81 of *Proceedings of Machine Learning Research*, pages 77–91. PMLR, 23–24 Feb.

Caliskan, A., Bryson, J. J., and Narayanan, A. (2017). Semantics derived automatically from language corpora contain human-like biases. *Science*, 356(6334):183–186.

Escudé Font, J., Costa-jussa, M., and R. (2019). Equalizing gender bias in neural machine translation with word embeddings techniques. In *Proceedings of the First Workshop on Gender Bias in Natural Language Processing*, pages 147–154, Florence, Italy, August. Association for Computational Linguistics.

Field, A., Blodgett, S. L., Waseem, Z., and Tsvetkov, Y. (2021). A survey of race, racism, and anti-racism in NLP. In *Proceedings of the 59th Annual Meeting of the Association for Computational Linguistics and the 11th International Joint Conference on Natural Language Processing (Volume 1: Long Papers)*, pages 1905–1925, Online, August. Association for Computational Linguistics.

Grave, E., Bojanowski, P., Gupta, P., Joulin, A., and Mikolov, T. (2018). Learning word vectors for 157 languages. In *Proceedings of the International Conference on Language Resources and Evaluation (LREC 2018)*.

Hanna, A., Denton, E., Smart, A., and Smith-Loud, J. (2020). Towards a critical race methodology in algorithmic fairness. FAT* '20, page 501–512, New York, NY, USA. Association for Computing Machinery.

Haokip, T. (2021). From 'chinky' to 'coronavirus': racism against northeast indians during the covid-19 pandemic. *Asian Ethnicity*, 22(2):353–373.

Hasanuzzaman, M., Dias, G., and Way, A. (2017). Demographic word embeddings for racism detection on Twitter. In *Proceedings of the Eighth International Joint Conference on Natural Language Processing (Volume 1: Long Papers)*, pages 926–936, Taipei, Taiwan, November.

Kaminsky; Long, R. D. (2011). *India Today: An Encyclopedia of Life in the Republic.* ABC-CLIO. ISBN 978-0-313-37463-0.

Manzini, T., Yao Chong, L., Black, A. W., and Tsvetkov, Y. (2019). Black is to criminal as caucasian is to police: Detecting and removing multiclass bias in word embeddings. In *Proceedings of the 2019 Conference of the North American Chapter of the Association for Computational Linguistics: Human Language Technologies, Volume 1 (Long and Short Papers)*, pages 615–621, Minneapolis, Minnesota, June. Association for Computational Linguistics.

Pinto, A. (2001). Un conference against racism: Is caste race? *Economic and Political Weekly*, 36(30):2817–2820.

Zhao, J., Wang, T., Yatskar, M., Ordonez, V., and Chang, K.-W. (2018). Gender bias in coreference resolution: Evaluation and debiasing methods. In *Proceedings of the 2018 Conference of the North American Chapter of the Association for Computational Linguistics: Human Language Technologies, Volume 2 (Short Papers)*, pages 15–20. Association for Computational Linguistics, June.

Zhou, P., Shi, W., Zhao, J., Huang, K.-H., Chen, M., Cotterell, R., and Chang, K.-W. (2019). Examining gender bias in languages with grammatical gender. In *Proceedings of the 2019 Conference on Empirical Methods in Natural Language Processing and the 9th International Joint Conference on Natural Language Processing (EMNLP-IJCNLP)*, pages 5276–5284, Hong Kong, China, November. Association for Computational Linguistics.

Proceedings of LATERAISSE Workshop @LREC2022, pages 8–16
Marseille, 25 June 2022
© European Language Resources Association (ELRA), licensed under CC-BY-NC-4.0

Objectifying Women? A Syntactic Bias in French and English Corpora.

Yanis da Cunha, Anne Abeillé
Laboratoire de Linguistique Formelle, Université Paris Cité
8, Rue Albert Einstein 75013 Paris
yanis.dc@gmail.com, anne.abeille@u-paris.fr

Abstract

Gender biases in syntax have been documented for languages with grammatical gender for cases where mixed-gender coordination structures take masculine agreement, or with male-first preference in the ordering of pairs (Adam and Eve). On the basis of various annotated corpora spanning different genres (fiction, newspapers, speech and web), we show another syntactic gender bias: masculine pronouns are more often subjects than feminine pronouns, in both English and French. We find the same bias towards masculine subjects for French human nouns, which then refer to males and females. Comparing the subject of passive verbs and the object of active verbs, we show that this syntactic function bias is not reducible to a bias in semantic role assignment since it is also found with non-agentive subjects. For French fiction, we also found that the masculine syntactic function bias is larger in text written by male authors – female authors seem to be unbiased. We finally discuss two principles as possible explanations, 'Like Me' and 'Easy first', and examine the effect of the discourse tendency for men being agents and topics. We conclude by addressing the impact of such biases in language technologies.

Keywords: corpus, gender bias, syntactic function, French, English, syntax, treebank

1. Introduction

Gender biases have been documented at various levels of grammar in various languages. Among others, there are biases in favor of the masculine in agreement, where coordinations of mixed genders generally trigger masculine agreement across languages (Corbett, 1983). Despite the possibility of closest conjunct agreement (An and Abeillé, 2021), masculine controllers therefore have a privileged status in agreement patterns. In word order, men generally appear before women in binomials in English (Mollin, 2013; Mollin, 2014) and French (mari et femme 'husband and wife', frères et soeurs 'brothers and sisters', Abeillé et al. (2018)). However, some reversals are attested (aunts and uncles, mother and father, (Goldberg and Lee, 2021)). Experiments on English showed that a men-first bias can also occur in sentence production (Brough et al., 2020). For semantic roles, psycholinguistic experiments on French and German showed that it is more expected for men to be agents than for women (Esaulova and Von Stockhausen, 2015). There is thus converging evidence, from experiments and corpora, that gender stereotypes and biases can affect linguistic patterns.

This paper aims to shed light on another type of gender bias, which affects syntactic function: men are more likely to be a syntactic subject than women. Such a bias has been noticed in examples used linguistics papers, both in English (Kotek et al., 2021; Cépeda et al., 2021) and in French (Richy and Burnett, 2020). For instance, in the linguistic examples of the French journal *Langue Française* (1969-1971 and 2008-1017), Richy and Burnett (2020) show that women represent 12% of subjects and 30% of objects, while men represent 88% of subjects but 70% of objects. This difference was significant, and year of publication and author gender did not play a role, suggesting that this gender bias is stable across time and authors. However, it can be asked whether this bias is specific to linguists' usage or whether it is a more general trend.

Such an effect of gender is reminiscent of the effect of animacy, definiteness, person or pronominality on syntactic functions. Studies from formalist (Aissen, 1999; Aissen, 2003; Jelinek and Carnie, 2003), typological (Haspelmath, 2021) and psycholinguistic (MacDonald, 2013; Lamers and De Swart, 2011) perspectives have shown that function coding is driven by hierarchically ordered information generally characterized as 'prominence features'. Such features can be represented in the form of scales (exemplified in 1), where > means 'more prominent than' .

(1) a. Animate > Inanimate
b. Definite > Indefinite
c. Pronoun > Noun

(2) Subject > Object

Scales like these formalize the fact that prominent referents are more likely to occupy more prominent functions (subjects) and less prominent referents tend to occupy less prominent functions (objects). Thus prominence scales in (1) tend to align with the syntactic function scale in (2). We will refer to animate, definite and pronominal subjects as 'aligned configurations' (prominent referents with a prominent function), while inanimate, indefinite and nominal subjects would be 'unaligned configurations'. This general effect shows up in two ways across languages (Bresnan et al., 2001). On one hand, prominence scales can induce strong grammaticality contrasts, bringing into play differential argument coding or obligatory voice alternations. For example, in Spanish or Hindi, animate objects have to be coded with an extra case marker, because animate objects do not represent an aligned configuration. On the other hand, prominence scales can induce production and processing preferences, making aligned configurations easier to predict and more frequent in corpora. Therefore, it has been noted in various languages that animate patients are more likely to be used as passive subjects, to favor an aligned animate-subject configuration, and avoid an unaligned animate-object configuration in active voice (for animacy effects in active/passive alternation see Tanaka et al. (2011) for Japanese, Hundt et al. (2021) for English, Thuilier et al. (2021; da Cunha and Abeillé (2020) for French).

Finding syntactic function gender biases in corpora would thus provide evidence for integrating gender information as a prominence feature, as suggested by Esaulova and Von Stockhausen (2015). This would have consequences for psychological and typological studies, where gender would have to be taken into account for its possible effects on syntactic patterns, but it would also highlight the importance of gender biases in language for language technologies. (Wisniewski et al., 2021; Sun et al., 2019; Costa-jussà, 2019; Brown et al., 2020).

Our first goal is thus to replicate the findings that men are more likely to be subjects in linguistic examples (Cépeda et al., 2021; Richy and Burnett, 2020; Kotek et al., 2021) for more genres : newspapers, fiction, speech and web language. In a second step, we will take into account semantic roles, topicality and author gender to explore possible explanations for a gender bias in syntactic function. We will then discuss on the possible integration of gender among prominence features.

2. Methodology

We aim to detect and compare syntactic function gender biases across languages and genres. We selected corpora both in French and English. In French, we used the French TreeBank (FTB) for the journalistic genre (Abeillé et al., 2019), using a version annotated for expletive subjects (Candito et al., 2014). For spontaneous speech, we used three corpora from the Orféo project (Benzitoun and Debaisieux, 2020), namely the CFFP, the CRFP and the C-Oral-Rom. For fiction, we selected novels from contemporary Frantext (ATILF, 2022) and for web French we used FrWac (Baroni et al., 2009). For English, we used the Universal Dependencies (UD) corpora annotated for genre. We selected the English Web Treebank (EWT) (Silveira et al., 2014), the Georgetown University Multilayer (GUM) corpus (Zeldes, 2017) (which contains various genres, among others : fiction, news, conversation, interviews...), the LinES corpus (Ahrenberg, 2015), from which we only kept literature, and finally the English portion of the Parallel Universal Dependencies (PUD) corpus (McDonald et al., 2013), from which we only kept news. The table 1 summarizes some information about the selected corpora.

Language	Genre	Corpus	Period
French	Newpapers	FTB	1900-1993
	Speech	Orféo	1994-2012
	Fiction	Frantext	1980-2021
	Web	FrWac	2010
English	Web	EWT	1999-2011
	Varied	GUM	2000-2020
	Fiction	Lines	1899-1998
	News	PUD	—

Table 1: Selected corpora

We extracted all subjects and objects from dependency-annotated corpora (FTB, Orféo corpora, UD English corpora). For French, we kept singular nouns and clitic pronouns (*il* 'he/it', *elle* 'she/it', *le* 'him/it', *la* 'her/it'), for English just singular pronouns (*he, him, she, her, it*). For FrWac and Frantext, which have no dependency annotation, we took sequences defined as : *no preposition + determiner + noun + conjugated verb + determiner + noun*. The *no preposition* condition filters out examples such as (3), where a preverbal noun (here, SG) is not a subject. This allows us to assume that preverbal nouns are subjects and postverbal ones are objects, as in (4). From Frantext and FrWac, we also took a sample of singular clitic pronouns (*il, elle, le la*), whose form already indicates their syntactic function.

(3) [...] le président de la SG [Société Générale] écarte l'idée d'un rapprochement avec BNP [Banque Nationale de Paris] Paribas (FrWac, efinancialcareers.fr)
'The president(MASC) of the SG(FEM) rules out the idea(FEM) of a merger with BNP Paribas'

(4) a. Votre fils apprendra la voltige (CHANDERNAGOR Françoise, L'Enfant des Lumières, 1995, Frantext)
'Your son(MASC) will learn aerobatics(FEM)'

b. La confédération assure le cadre permanent de discussion et d'action [...] (FrWac, gauchepopulaire.fr)
'The confederation(FEM) provides the permanent framework(MASC) for discussion and action'

The FTB annotation allows us to filter out expletive subjects *il* and predicative complements. For other French corpora, we removed the most frequent impersonal and predicative verbs according to the FTB : *falloir* 'to be necessary', *être* 'to be', *rester* 'to remain', *devenir* 'to become', *sembler* 'to seem', *paraître* 'to look like'. We only kept singular nouns, to avoid mixed-gender and generic forms. To do so, we removed lemmas whose token contains an additional *-s*, which is a plural marker in French. With regard to gender annotation, the situation is different for nouns and pronouns. French and English pronouns provide grammatical and social gender information respectively. For French nouns, the FTB is already annotated for grammatical gender. For the other corpora, we annotated grammatical gender for all nouns using information available in Flexique (Bonami et al., 2014), a French dictionary which provides grammatical gender information for 31 000 nouns. Finally, we annotated animacy (human, animate, inanimate) using an animacy-annotated version of Flexique (Bonami, p.c.). The table 2 shows our annotated data set. For French nouns, 73% of the whole data set has been annotated for grammatical gender and 70% for animacy (human vs inanimate nouns). Only the annotated data is reported there. It can be seen that English has much fewer data points than French, but excepts for FrWac (web) and Frantext (fiction), this is due to corpus size.

3. Results

3.1. Syntactic Function Bias across Genres

We first report results for English, in figure 1. Masculine bias can be seen in two ways. First, it appears that masculine pronouns are always more frequent than feminine ones, independently of syntactic function. For example, fiction contains 112 masculine pronouns but only 57 feminine ones. This imbalance is consistent across genres, but less strong in speech. Secondly, aside from being rarer, feminine pronouns also appear more often as objects than masculine one. This can be seen by the height of the orange areas. We can also see that within objects *'it'*, the inanimate pronoun, is the most frequent, followed by feminine pronouns and finally masculine pronouns. Masculine pronouns are thus more often subjects (height of the blue areas). The less biased genre seems to be speech, where feminine and masculine pronouns are almost equally frequent, and where there does not seem to be a syntactic function bias. We thus see a tendency for masculine pronouns to be subjects across genres, generalizing previous results found in linguistic examples to the whole of the English language (Kotek et al., 2021; Cépeda et al., 2021).

We can compare these results with those for French clitic pronouns, in figure 2. We find again that masculine pronouns are more frequent than feminine ones, but the bias for masculine pronouns to be subjects does not appear as clearly. All genres show slightly more masculine pronouns as subjects, except for newspapers where the bias is reversed. The main problem here is that contrary to English pronouns, French pronouns do not reflect social gender but grammatical gender. As a consequence, French pronouns are not specified for animacy, they may either refer to humans or to inanimates, as in (5). If social gender plays a role in syntactic function assignment, it would do so only for humans, where grammatical gender is interpreted as social gender in most cases (Richy and Burnett, 2021).

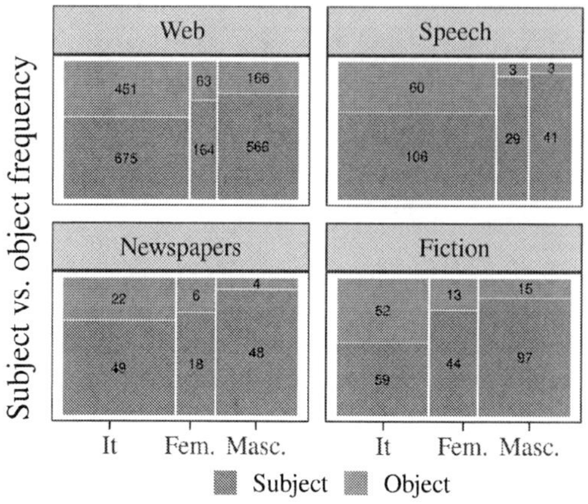

Figure 1: Gender and function frequencies for English personal pronouns

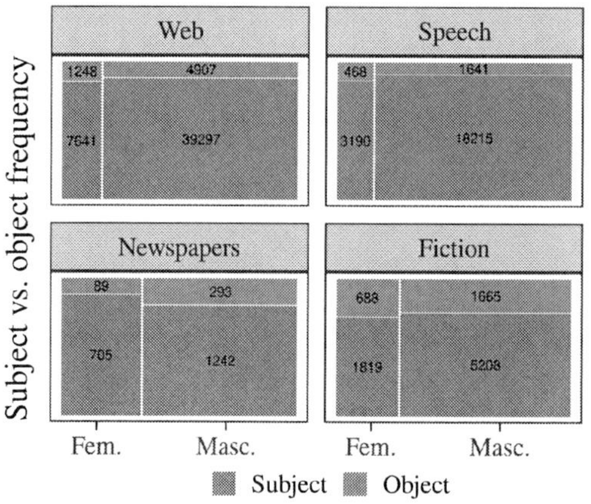

Figure 2: Gender and function frequencies for French clitic pronouns

(5) Mais je veux dire la gestion$_i$ de la ville est relativement bonne [...] Elle$_i$ correspond au type de population qui réside à Montreuil.
'But I mean, the management(FEM)$_i$ of the city is relatively good. It(FEM)$_i$ corresponds to the type of population that lives in Montreuil'

To reduce noise, we can look at the subject bias for nouns, for which we have animacy and grammatical gender information. Figure 3 shows the frequency in subject function by gender and animacy of French nouns. Error bars indicate standard error. We can now see a difference between inanimate and human nouns. On one hand, feminine and masculine inanimates do not differ in their frequency as subject (only fiction texts show a slightly greater frequency for feminine noun subjects). On the other hand masculine humans, ie. men, show a bias toward subject function and are thus more often subjects than feminine humans, ie. women. This difference between masculine and femi-

	Fiction	Newspapers	Web	Speech	Total
English pronouns	280	147	2085	242	2754
French pronouns	9380	2329	53093	23514	88316
French nouns	20444	16489	115059	21862	173854
Total	30104	18965	170237	45618	264924

Table 2: Composition of the studied sample

nine human nouns can be seen for each genre except for fiction, where the bias is less strong. This result indicates that gender in French does indeed have a different impact on syntactic function use for inanimate and human nouns, since it matters for the latter but not the former (as supported by Richy and Burnett (2021) among others). As inanimate nouns are not biased for syntactic function, it corroborates the idea that their grammatical gender is not interpreted in the same way as the grammatical gender of human nouns. However we do not claim that grammatical gender of inanimate nouns could not be interpreted at all (see Williams et al. (2021 03 17) for a discussion). For what concerns syntactic function, it is clear that French human nouns show the same pattern as English pronouns, where masculines are more frequently subjects, which is evidence for a similar impact of social gender.

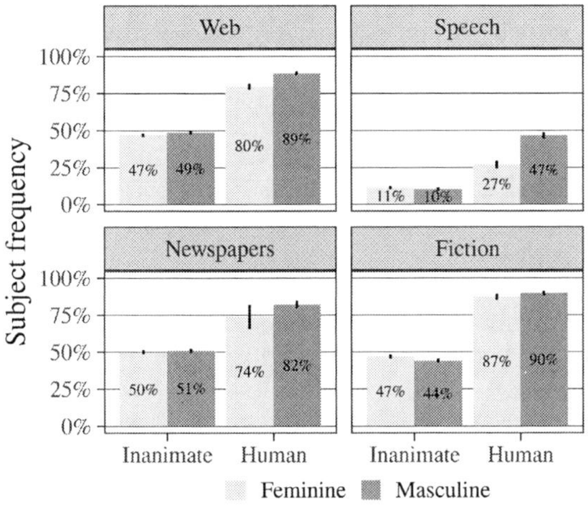

Figure 3: Subject frequency of French singular nouns according to grammatical gender and animacy

There appears to be a bias for men being subjects more frequently than women, both in French (human nouns) and in English (human pronouns). We can now compare these two languages across genres. Figure 4 shows the strength of masculines-as-subjects bias in the four genres we studied. Our bias measure corresponds to the difference between masculine subject frequency and feminine subject frequency. As a consequence, the greater this difference is, the more men are found as subjects compared to women. For example, English fiction has a bias of 10 points. So, masculine subject frequency in English fiction (86%) is 10 points higher than feminine subject frequency (76%). We established this measure to allow easier comparisons of gender biases in syntactic functions between genres and languages.

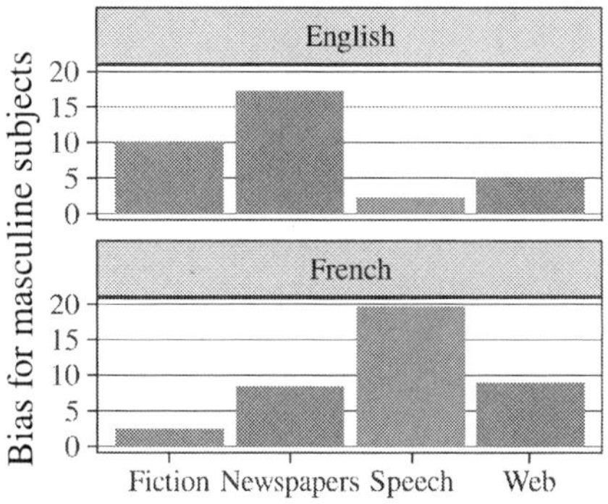

Figure 4: Bias for masculine subjects across genres in English (personal pronouns) and French (human nouns). The bias measure indicates to what extent masculines are more frequently subjects than feminines.

We show that English narrative genres (fiction and newspapers) have a rather strong bias for masculine subjects (10 points or more). Interactive genres (speech, web) are less biased (less than 5 points). In French such a generalization seems not to hold : newspapers and web both show a moderate bias (about 8 points) and speech shows the strongest one (20 points). This time, fiction shows no bias (just 2.5 points). Although there seems to be a bias across genres, we do not see a clear link between the type of genre and the strength of its masculine subject bias. A general conclusion we can draw is that the type of function bias noticed in linguistic examples in French and English papers (Richy and Burnett, 2020; Kotek et al., 2021; Cépeda et al., 2021) is not genre-specific but reflects a general trend in other genres both in English and French.

Through this method, we can ask whether this bias for masculine subjects is due to syntax and/or to other factors such as semantic role and discourse. Indeed, subjects are prototypical agents and topics while objects are prototypical patients, which could explain the syntactic biases we observe. To investigate this, we looked at semantic roles and pronominalization rate of masculine and feminine subjects and objects.

3.2. Syntactic Bias and Semantic Roles

We aim to investigate whether gender biases remain after taking semantic roles into account. To probe this, we compare subjects of passive verbs and objects of active verbs (which bear the same patient-like roles) with subjects of active verbs (which are more agent-like). Assuming that active objects and passive subjects may both bear the same patient-like roles, observing gender to have a differential effect on the two syntactic functions conditional on the same semantic role would indicate that the gender bias goes beyond semantics. In the case of the active/passive alternation, the difference between subjects and objects is indeed more closely related to syntax, and information structure, than to semantics.

For this part of the study, we only consider at corpora annotated for passive : FTB and English UD corpora. As we lack data for human feminine nouns in French (only 6 passive subjects), we report all data for French nouns and pronouns, including data points for which animacy was not provided by Flexique. We may take animacy into account for future research.

Figure 5 summarizes our results. It shows that both in English and French, objects are more often feminine and active subjects are more often masculine. Passive subjects, which share syntactic properties with active subjects and semantic properties with objects, are an in-between case : they are more often masculine than objects, but less often than active subjects. The difference between objects and subjects in general echoes the differences seen in the previous section (3.1). It is to be noted that English pronoun gender represents social gender (men vs. women), while for French pronouns and nouns, gender is grammatical gender, which is correlated but not equivalent to social gender. We hypothesize that the difference observed in French is due to social gender, but we leave the testing of this hypothesis for future work.

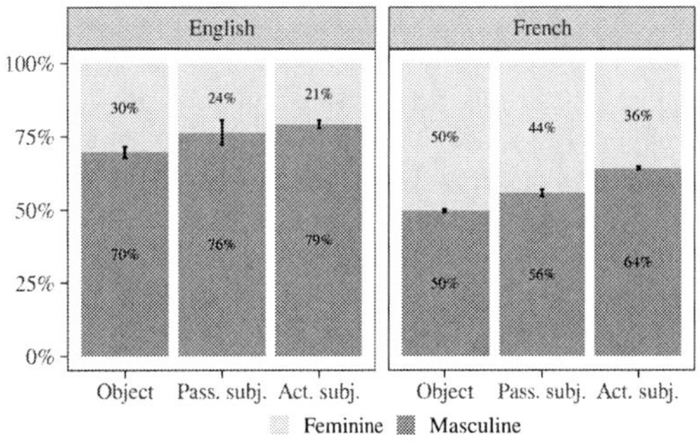

Figure 5: Proportions of masculine and feminine referents according to their syntactic function for English pronouns and French FTB pronouns and nouns, comparing transitive active and intransitive passive.

These results bring new evidence for a gender bias in syntactic functions which is not completely reducible to semantic roles. Indeed, even if objects and passive subjects both bear patient-like roles, we still observe a bias for masculine subjects, suggesting that the syntactic function bias is not due to semantics only. We showed that there is a superadditive effect between semantics and syntax: active subjects are even more often masculine than passive subjects. So there is also a bias for masculines to be agents. This result is consistent with previous literature based on linguistic examples (Kotek et al., 2021; Richy and Burnett, 2020; Cépeda et al., 2021), and we now show that it holds in other genres.

We thus showed that with constant semantic role, a bias for masculine subjects still appears. Gender biases we observed in syntactic functions cannot be explained only by a discourse tendency for men to be agents more frequently than women.

3.3. Syntactic Bias and Topicality

Another factor we now have to explore is topicality, which could also explain the observed pattern. Topicality can be assessed in various ways. We adopt here a definition in terms of topic-worthiness (Dalrymple and Nikolaeva, 2011) or Topic Accessibility Scale (Lambrecht, 1996), that is to say the likelihood of being a good topic candidate. One of the criteria for topicality is being a pronoun, since pronouns encode active referents in the discourse universe. In linguistic examples, it has been found that men are more often referred to by pronouns than women (Richy and Burnett, 2021; Cépeda et al., 2021; Kotek et al., 2021). We thus looked at the pronominalization rate of masculine and feminine referents across genres. Figure 6 presents our results.

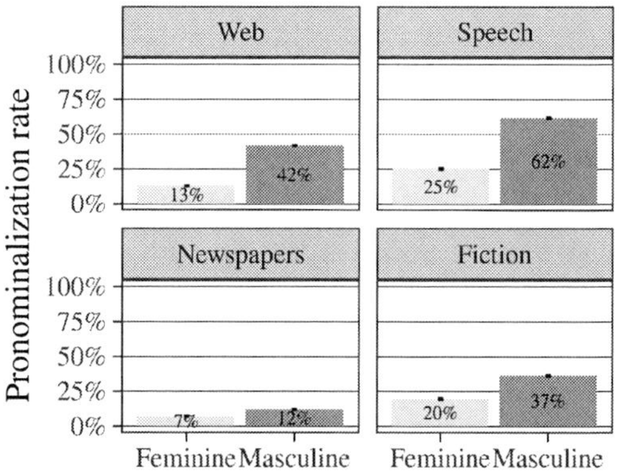

Figure 6: Pronominalization rate for masculine and feminine referents in French corpora.

We show that in the four genres under consideration, feminine referents are less often coded as pronouns than masculine ones. The less biased genre are newspapers, but French newspapers in general use fewer pronouns (Poiret and Liu, 2020). On the contrary, speech shows the greatest difference, because spoken language uses more pronouns (*Ibid.*). The main consequence of this imbalance would be that masculine referents are more often topics than feminine referents. Yet, as subjects are canonical topics (Lambrecht, 1996; Givón, 1983), it would imply that subjects are more often masculine, and that the syntactic function gender bias may be reduced to this. We discuss such a hypothesis in the last section (4)

3.4. Syntactic Bias and Speaker Gender

Finally we investigate whether speaker gender plays a role: is masculine subject bias a male speaker tendency, like a *'Me-First' principle* (Cooper and Ross, 1975) or a *'Like Me' effect* (Brough et al., 2020) ? or is it a more general bias shared by male and female speakers ? For English linguistic examples, (Kotek et al., 2021) showed that author gender plays a role in gender biases, but not for French linguistic examples (Richy and Burnett, 2020). A *'Like Me' effect* in gender biases in syntax would thus constitute another type of explanation for the observed pattern.
Here, we only look at the data from the Frantext corpus (French, fiction), which is annotated for speaker gender. We aim to see whether the syntactic bias for masculine subjects highlighted until now depends on the gender of the speaker. Figure 7 reports our results.

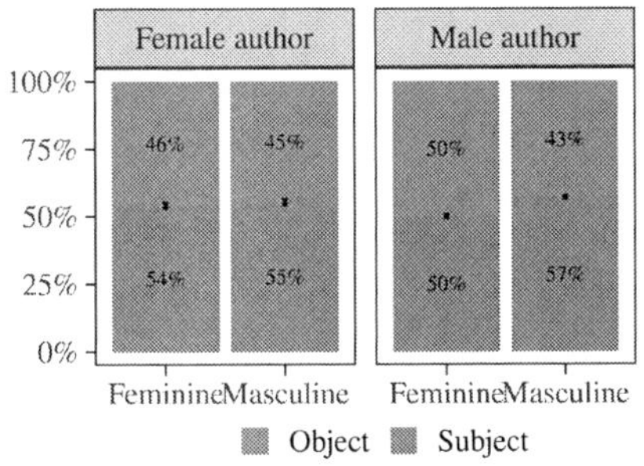

Figure 7: Proportions of subjects and objects according to speaker and noun gender in French fiction.

Whereas female authors do not show a difference between masculine and feminine nouns for subject and object frequencies (more or less 55% for both), male authors do show a difference. For them, masculine nouns are more often subjects (57%) than feminine ones (50%). Thus, a syntactic bias for masculine subjects seems to hold only for male authors here.
We analyze these data to test significance of the interaction between author and noun gender with a logistic regression model (package *lme4* on R (Bates et al., 2014)). We use function as predicted variable (*Subject* = 1, *Object* = 0), author and noun gender as predictors (which we normalized), with their interaction, and noun lemma and author as random variables, with random intercepts only. Table 3 presents our results. We find a significant effect of noun gender ($E = 0.11$; $SE = 0.03$; $p < 0.001$) : masculine nouns are more likely to be subjects than feminine ones. We do not find an effect for author gender ($p > 0.05$) but there is a significant interaction between author and noun gender ($E = 0.04$; $SE = 0.02$; $p < 0.05$). The effect of noun gender thus significantly interacts with author gender : noun gender only matters for male authors, who use masculine subjects more frequently.
One interesting consequence of this result is that it partially corresponds to a *'Like-Me' effect*. Indeed men do tend to use masculines as subjects. But why don't women use more feminines as subjects ? It would be interesting to study this type of interaction between speaker gender and gender syntactic biases for other languages and genres, taking into account animacy.

4. Discussion & conclusion

We found a gender bias in syntactic functions in both English and French across different genres: female referents (French human nouns and English pronouns) are less likely to be subjects than male referents. In French, we showed how this bias interacts with animacy, since grammatical gender has an effect only for human referents. We saw that the strength of the masculine bias for subjects is not clearly linked to genre characteristics (narrative, interactive etc).
We also explore two possible explanations for this bias : if men are more often subjects, it would come from other properties of subjects, like being canonical agents and topics. Discourse tendencies for men to be agents and topics would then be a source for syntactic biases. We showed that, although masculine referents are indeed more often agents, the syntactic bias goes beyond semantics, since it holds even when semantic roles are kept constant. If one considers only patientive referents (objects and passive subjects), a bias towards masculine subjects remains. For topicality, we found that feminine referents are indeed less referred to via pronouns. As pronouns encode active referents, they are more topical, and thus more often found as subjects, the canonical topics. Controlling for available topics in a text would be useful to corroborate this hypothesis, in a similar way to what Huet et al. (2013) did for French newspapers. Huet et al. (2013) showed that in the French journal *Le Monde* (from which the FTB, used in our study, was extracted), in 1985 (five years before the FTB), only 10% of the articles mentioned women, while 50% of them mentioned men (Huet et al., 2013). If most human referents in a text are men, it is not surprising to find them more often as subjects, since human subjects are canonical topics/agents. Nevertheless, we observe the same type of bias in other genres, including speech, which may not have the same referents as newspapers.
Finally, we investigate the possibility that gender biases are due to a kind of *'Me-First' principle* or *'Like Me'*

	Estimate	Std. deviation	*z-value*	*p-value*
Intercept	0.18	0.03	5.59	< 0.001
Masculine vs. feminin noun	0.11	0.03	3.82	0.00014
Male vs. female author	-0.03	0.02	-1.33	0.18282
Interaction	0.05	0.02	2.93	0.00334

Table 3: Logistic regression modeling syntactic function with the interaction between speaker and noun gender (number of data points = 21 995).

effect (Cooper and Ross, 1975; Brough et al., 2020), which makes speakers produce/process referents they identify with more easily. In French fiction, which was the least biased genre in our cross-genre comparison (Figure 4), female and male authors behave differently. Indeed, only male authors exhibit a bias for masculine subjects, which supports a general idea of a *'Like Me' effect* (Brough et al., 2020). However, women showed a rather unbiased usage in our data, casting doubt on this conclusion.
More generally, among semantic roles, topicality or *'Like Me'* effects, disentangling syntactic biases from other kinds of gender bias will be necessary to find explanations for them.

Therefore our work extends literature on gender biases in syntax, showing that it holds across genres. It also opens the question of whether the discourse tendency of masculine subjects and feminine objects could be formalized into a gender prominence scale like that of animacy, definiteness or person prominence. It would then be take the form of the following scale (6), which tend to be aligned with the syntactic function scale.

(6) Masculine > feminine
Subject > object

The gender bias we found thus seems comparable to other preferences in function assignment. These preferences can be summarized by the *Easy first* principle, which states that referents "important or conceptually salient to the speaker" and "more easily retrieved from memory" tend to appear earlier or as subjects in a sentence (MacDonald, 2013, 3). Investigating whether male referents can be considered as "easier" for some speakers (taking speaker gender into account), would lead to a better understanding of the gender biases we found.
We finally point out that it's important to detect gender biases of this kind since they have an impact on language technologies : they can be learned by neural models (Brown et al., 2020) and can yield to biases in NLP tasks such as automatic translation (Wisniewski et al., 2021; Sun et al., 2019; Costa-jussà, 2019).

5. References

Abeillé, A., An, A., and Shiraïshi, A. (2018). L'accord de proximité du déterminant en français. *Discours. Revue de linguistique, psycholinguistique et informatique. A journal of linguistics, psycholinguistics and computational linguistics*, (22).

Abeillé, A., Clément, L., and Liégeois, L. (2019). Un corpus arboré pour le français: le french treebank. *Traitement Automatique des Langues*, 60(2):19–43.

Ahrenberg, L. (2015). Converting an english-swedish parallel treebank to universal dependencies. In *Proceedings of the Third International Conference on Dependency Linguistics (Depling 2015)*, pages 10–19.

Aissen, J. (1999). Markedness and subject choice in optimality theory. *Natural Language & Linguistic Theory*, 17(4):673–711.

Aissen, J. (2003). Differential object marking: Iconicity vs. economy. *Natural Language & Linguistic Theory*, 21(3):435–483.

An, A. and Abeillé, A. (2021). Closest conjunct agreement with attributive adjectives. *Journal of French Language Studies*, pages 1–28. Publisher: Cambridge University Press.

ATILF. (2022). Base textuelle frantext (online). Accessed: 2022-04-05.

Baroni, M., Bernardini, S., Ferraresi, A., and Zanchetta, E. (2009). The wacky wide web: a collection of very large linguistically processed web-crawled corpora. *Language resources and evaluation*, 43(3):209–226.

Bates, D., Mächler, M., Bolker, B., and Walker, S. (2014). Fitting linear mixed-effects models using lme4. *arXiv preprint arXiv:1406.5823*.

Benzitoun, C. and Debaisieux, J.-M. (2020). Orféo: un corpus et une plateforme pour l'étude du français contemporain.

Bonami, O., Caron, G., and Plancq, C. (2014). Construction d'un lexique flexionnel phonétisé libre du français. In *SHS Web of Conferences*, volume 8, pages 2583–2596. EDP Sciences.

Bresnan, J., Dingare, S., and Manning, C. D. (2001). Soft constraints mirror hard constraints: Voice and person in english and lummi. In *Proceedings of the LFG01 Conference*, pages 13–32. Stanford: CSLI Publications.

Brough, J., Branigan, H., Harris, L., and Rabagliati, H. (2020). The influence of race and gender on perspective-taking during language production.

Brown, T. B., Mann, B., Ryder, N., Subbiah, M.,

Kaplan, J., Dhariwal, P., Neelakantan, A., Shyam, P., Sastry, G., and Askell, A. (2020). Language models are few-shot learners. *arXiv preprint arXiv:2005.14165*.

Candito, M., Perrier, G., Guillaume, B., Ribeyre, C., Fort, K., Seddah, D., and de La Clergerie, E. V. (2014). Deep syntax annotation of the sequoia french treebank. In *International Conference on Language Resources and Evaluation (LREC)*.

Cooper, W. E. and Ross, J. R. (1975). World order. *Papers from the parasession on functionalism*, pages 63–111.

Corbett, G. (1983). Resolution rules: agreement in person, number, and gender. *Order, concord and constituency*, pages 175–206. Publisher: Foris Publications Dordrecht.

Costa-jussà, M. R. (2019). An analysis of gender bias studies in natural language processing. *Nature Machine Intelligence*, 1(11):495–496. Publisher: Nature Publishing Group.

Cépeda, P., Kotek, H., Pabst, K., and Syrett, K. (2021). Gender bias in linguistics textbooks: Has anything changed since macaulay & brice 1997? *Language*. Publisher: Linguistic Society of America.

da Cunha, Y. and Abeillé, A. (2020). L'alternance actif/passif en français: une étude statistique sur corpus écrit. *Discours. Revue de linguistique, psycholinguistique et informatique. A journal of linguistics, psycholinguistics and computational linguistics*, (27).

Dalrymple, M. and Nikolaeva, I. (2011). *Objects and information structure*. Number 131. Cambridge University Press.

Esaulova, Y. and Von Stockhausen, L. (2015). Crosslinguistic evidence for gender as a prominence feature. *Frontiers in Psychology*, 6. Publisher: Frontiers.

Givón, T. (1983). *Topic continuity in discourse*. Amsterdam: John Benjamins.

Goldberg, A. E. and Lee, C. (2021). Accessibility and historical change: An emergent cluster led uncles and aunts to become aunts and uncles. *Frontiers in psychology*, 12:1418. Publisher: Frontiers.

Haspelmath, M. (2021). Role-reference associations and the explanation of argument coding splits. *Linguistics*, 59(1):123–174.

Huet, T., Biega, J., and Suchanek, F. M. (2013). Mining history with le monde. In *Proceedings of the 2013 workshop on Automated knowledge base construction - AKBC '13*, pages 49–54. ACM Press.

Hundt, M., Röthlisberger, M., and Seoane, E. (2021). Predicting voice alternation across academic englishes. *Corpus Linguistics and Linguistic Theory*, 17(1):189–222.

Jelinek, E. and Carnie, A. (2003). Argument hierarchies and the mapping principle. In *In Festschrift for Jelinek*.

Kotek, H., Dockum, R., Babinski, S., and Geissler, C. (2021). Gender bias and stereotypes in linguistic example sentences. *Language*. Publisher: Linguistic Society of America.

Lambrecht, K. (1996). *Information structure and sentence form: Topic, focus, and the mental representations of discourse referents*, volume 71. Cambridge university press.

Lamers, M. and De Swart, P. (2011). *Case, word order and prominence: Interacting cues in language production and comprehension*, volume 40. Springer Science & Business Media.

MacDonald, M. C. (2013). How language production shapes language form and comprehension. *Frontiers in psychology*, 4:226.

McDonald, R., Nivre, J., Quirmbach-Brundage, Y., Goldberg, Y., Das, D., Ganchev, K., Hall, K., Petrov, S., Zhang, H., Täckström, O., Bedini, C., Bertomeu Castelló, N., and Lee, J. (2013). Universal Dependency annotation for multilingual parsing. In *Proceedings of the 51st Annual Meeting of the Association for Computational Linguistics (Volume 2: Short Papers)*, pages 92–97, Sofia, Bulgaria, August. Association for Computational Linguistics.

Mollin, S. (2013). Pathways of change in the diachronic development of binomial reversibility in late modern american english. *Journal of English Linguistics*, 41(2):168–203. Publisher: Sage Publications Sage CA: Los Angeles, CA.

Mollin, S. (2014). *The (ir) reversibility of English binomials: Corpus, constraints, developments*, volume 64. John Benjamins Publishing Company.

Poiret, R. and Liu, H. (2020). Some quantitative aspects of written and spoken french based on syntactically annotated corpora. *Journal of French Language Studies*, 30(3):355–380.

Richy, C. and Burnett, H. (2020). Jean does the dishes while marie fixes the car: a qualitative and quantitative study of social gender in french syntax articles. *Journal of French Language Studies*, 30(1):47–72. Publisher: Cambridge University Press.

Richy, C. and Burnett, H. (2021). Démêler les effets des stéréotypes et le genre grammatical dans le biais masculin: une approche expérimentale. *GLAD!. Revue sur le langage, le genre, les sexualités*, (10).

Silveira, N., Dozat, T., de Marneffe, M.-C., Bowman, S., Connor, M., Bauer, J., and Manning, C. D. (2014). A gold standard dependency corpus for English. In *Proceedings of the Ninth International Conference on Language Resources and Evaluation (LREC-2014)*.

Sun, T., Gaut, A., Tang, S., Huang, Y., ElSherief, M., Zhao, J., Mirza, D., Belding, E., Chang, K.-W., and Wang, W. Y. (2019). Mitigating gender bias in natural language processing: Literature review. *arXiv preprint arXiv:1906.08976*.

Tanaka, M. N., Branigan, H. P., McLean, J. F., and Pickering, M. J. (2011). Conceptual influences on word order and voice in sentence production: Evidence from japanese. *Journal of Memory and Language*, 65(3):318–330.

Thuilier, J., Grant, M., Crabbé, B., and Abeillé, A. (2021). Word order in french: the role of animacy. *Glossa: a journal of general linguistics*, 6(1).

Williams, A., Cotterell, R., Wolf-Sonkin, L., Blasi, D., and Wallach, H. (2021-03-17). On the relationships between the grammatical genders of inanimate nouns and their co-occurring adjectives and verbs. *Transactions of the Association for Computational Linguistics*, 9:139–159.

Wisniewski, G., Zhu, L., Ballier, N., and Yvon, F. (2021). Biais de genre dans un système de traduction automatique neuronale : une étude préliminaire. In *Actes de la 28e Conférence sur le Traitement Automatique des Langues Naturelles. Volume 1: conférence principale*, pages 11–25.

Zeldes, A. (2017). The GUM corpus: Creating multilayer resources in the classroom. *Language Resources and Evaluation*, 51(3):581–612.

Proceedings of LATERAISSE Workshop @LREC2022, pages 17–25
Marseille, 25 June 2022
© European Language Resources Association (ELRA), licensed under CC-BY-NC-4.0

A Cancel Culture Corpus through the lens of Natural Language Processing

Justus-Jonas Erker [1], Catalina Goanta [2], Gerasimos Spanakis [1]
[1] Maastricht University, [2] Utrecht University
{j.erker@student., jerry.spanakis@}maastrichtuniversity.nl
e.c.goanta@uu.nl

Abstract

Cancel Culture as an Internet phenomenon has been previously explored from a social and legal science perspective. This paper demonstrates how Natural Language Processing tasks can be derived from this previous work, underlying techniques on how cancel culture can be measured, identified and evaluated. As part of this paper, we introduce a first cancel culture data set with of over 2.3 million tweets and a framework to enlarge it further. We provide a detailed analysis of this data set and propose a set of features, based on various models including sentiment analysis and emotion detection that can help characterizing cancel culture.

Keywords: Social Media Analysis, Sentiment Analysis, Offensive Language Detection, Hate Speech Detection, Irony Detection, Emotion Detection, Cancel Culture

1. Introduction

Cancel culture is a phenomenon inherently linked to the Internet (Romano, 2019) that generally refers to the situation where an individual is 'professionally assassinated' (Carr, 2020). Unlike a movement, cancel culture on social media has 'neither leaders nor membership' (Mishan, 2020), but has rather emerged from earlier offline practices of public shaming such as call-out culture, boycotting (Mishan, 2020) or banishment (Kato, 2020) by attributing new meaning to terms (e.g. to cancel) cultivated in popular culture (Romano, 2019). Yet on the Internet, public shaming developed its own specific expressions, whether called 'the human flesh search engine' in the East (Shen, 2017) or 'cancel culture' in the West.

The resulting concept has a fuzzy meaning, challenging the limits of free speech on the one hand (Shen, 2017) and defamation on the other (Carr, 2020). Anyone can get cancelled, whether they are an online (e.g. Youtuber) or offline (e.g. politician) personality (Zurcher, 2021); whether they are a celebrity or an average citizen (Thomas, 2020). In addition, debates labeled as cancel culture have equally focused on non-human targets, such as children's books (Cantrell and Bickle, 2021).

The social justice aspects of cancel culture have raised acclaim in both popular and scientific literature. For instance, according to (Clark, 2020), 'cancel culture' reflects a critique of systemic inequality which has democratized public discourse. At the same time, given its virality, the concept transcended the queer communities of color it is said to have originated from (Clark, 2020), and has been used to often double as a mob intimidation technique (Romano, 2019). The gains and perils arising out of cancel culture very much depend on how this concept is framed. So far, academic scholarship investigated this phenomenon almost exclusively from a social science perspective, emphasizing power narratives connected to theoretical frameworks in critical studies (Bouvier and Machin, 2021) (Clark, 2020) (Veil and Waymer, 2021). As social media platforms are increasingly called upon to comply with state-mandated standards of content regulation, it is important to understand how cancel culture can be defined and measured.

This paper contributes to the debate by unpacking cancel culture and proposing a taxonomy of constitutive elements. Based on these elements, we propose a translation into a cohesive framework based on a collection of NLP tasks, which is currently missing from interdisciplinary as well as computational literature. We provide a detailed analysis of these measurements. Furthermore, we introduce a dataset of 22 cancel culture cases with over 2.3 million tweets, a data collection technique and a framework for enlarging this data set in the future. We discuss limitations of the proposed data gathering techniques as well as the limitations of measurements. With contributing this first data set, we hope to tackle these limitations in the future to get even more insights of cancel culture from an empirical perspective. To summarize, we investigate 2 research questions:

1. Can cancel culture incidents on Twitter be identified?
2. Can data gathering for cancel culture incidents be automated?

The paper is structured as follows: the first part of the paper describes the phenomena of cancel culture and maps it to a cohesive framework based on a collection of NLP tasks in §2. We describe our data collection technique in §3, followed by the description of our used features in §4. Based on these features, we investigate cancel culture in §5 and build our mathematical framework for enlarging the provided data set in §6. Following, we will discuss and wrap up the results in §7 and §8.

2. Theoretical Framework

This section describes the current work and how the characteristics of cancel culture can be mapped to NLP tasks.

2.1. Characteristics of Cancel Culture: A definitional overview

Given its varied usage, 'there is no single accepted definition of cancel culture' (Gerstmann, 2020). Mainstream media accounts have tried to pinpoint at the meaning of this phenomenon by framing it alongside moral lines, such as 'the public shaming of those deemed moral transgressors' (Mishan, 2020), or by focusing on the speakers: 'it is about unaccountable groups successfully applying pressure to punish someone for perceived wrong opinions.' (Gerstmann, 2020). Social science has led to more granular definitions. (Thomas, 2020) defines cancel culture as 'a way to call on others to reject a person or business', which can occur 'when the target breaks social norms - for example, making sexist comments - but it has also happened when people have expressed opinions on politics, business and even pop culture.' Focusing on a range of triggering causes for social justice, Ng portrays cancel culture as 'the withdrawal of any kind of support (viewership, social media follows, purchases of products endorsed by the person, etc.) for those who are assessed to have said or done something unacceptable or highly problematic, generally from a social justice perspective especially alert to sexism, heterosexism, homophobia, racism, bullying, and related issues.' Ng (2020). To 'cancel' a speaker has also been framed as 'an expression of agency, a choice to withdraw one's attention from someone or something whose values, (in)action, or speech are so offensive, one no longer wishes to grace them with their presence, time, and money.' (Clark, 2020; Bouvier and Machin, 2021). More succinctly, (Randall, 2021) believes the phenomenon to be a 'modern form of ostracism and harassment', while (Velasco, 2020) describes it as 'a sporadic collective social movement leveled against individuals who infringe on the loose norms of social acceptability'.

The range of definitions explored above generally converges on a few key components: the target committing a perceived social wrong, the cause relating to justice, and the call to withdrawing support. From this perspective, cancel culture represents a unilateral act in that it does not entail 'hearing and analyzing multiple and competing voices' in the context of conflicting moral values (Veil and Waymer, 2021).

2.2. Unpacking Cancel Culture

As indicated above, social science literature has so far focused on the social justice narratives behind cancel culture, to justify it as an expression of empowerment in the face of systemic inequality and unfairness. Given its significant legal and economical consequences, it is essential to contribute to existing discussions by identifying the constitutive characteristics of this complex socio-cultural phenomenon as it unfolds on social media. We therefore propose an original taxonomy which allows for a closer examination of the various aspects of cancel culture as outlined in popular depictions of its definition and scope.

Overall, we identified five main constitutive characteristics of cancel culture:

- **The target**: This is the object of cancel culture, and it covers a wide range of options. Not only individuals can be cancelled, but also businesses, and things such as children's books (Helmore, 2021) or other cultural products such as movies (Provost, 2020).
- **The ad hoc swarm**: This reflects the critical voices engaged in cancelling the target. Unlike coordinated raids organized on specific platforms (e.g. 4chan) and executed on others (Hine et al., 2017), cancel culture entails a more organic expression of moral righteousness (Chiou, 2020).
- **Perceived wrong**: This is the action (or inaction) perceived by the swarm as morally or legally unjust, and it also comes with a presumption of guilt attributed to the target.
- **Cause**: This reflects the nature of the perceived wrong as a type of injustice grave enough to the swarm to merit collective action.
- **Demands/actions**: This is the justice goal pursued by the swarm, a finality that is aimed as a punishment for the perceived wrong, and it can range from asking for someone to be fired, for a certain action to stop (e.g. not displaying a movie on Netflix). The demands pursued by the swarm are intended to bring attention to the perceived wrong, and in doing so, exercising pressure through comments, trending hashtags, etc.

2.3. Towards NLP Tasks

Based on the proposed taxonomy of the constitutive characteristics of cancel culture, we propose a series of NLP tasks that will be described in the following.

2.3.1. Text Classification

As explained in §2.1 a major characteristic of cancel culture is the targeting of an entity with a call to action for perceived wrong expressed in language. In the context of cancel culture, this language has been shown to be tending towards negative emotions and in some situations even hate speech (Hooks, 2020, p. 21, 36). Depending on the domain and the corresponding audience (which will differ by average age, interests, etc.) of a potentially canceled entity, a wide range of different language forms is to be expected. Therefore, being able to classify certain types of speech and sentiments of the language, and detecting possible anomalies along a certain time period can be expected to support detecting cancel culture events.

2.3.2. Actor Analysis (Target Filtering)

Since cancel culture demands a target, actor analysis could be used to filter out tweets that do not concern a specific target. While Named Entity Recognition could be helpful for this, it is most convenient to just filter for tweets that mention/target the entity in question directly.

2.3.3. Action Analysis

Another big part defined in §2.1 is the presence of demand for action. As this demand can be very broad depending on the domain in which an entity and its community are operating in, a possible solution is extraction of verbs using a Part-of-Speech (POS) tagger, and using a statistical model to count the frequent use of negative verbs (such as fired, resign, etc.) that might indicate cancel culture.

3. Data Collection

As part of this paper, a set of cancel culture cases from Twitter has been collected. The dataset is available on a GitHub repository [1] with the necessary data statements (Bender and Friedman, 2018). Furthermore, we provide a detailed description of the data set in the Appendix C. To ensure the quality of the data set, we have derived, based on §2.1, the following collection procedure.

3.1. Cancel Culture and Google Trends

As previously described, some components of cancel culture like the ad hoc swarm can not be seen as an attribute with some threshold that leads to a binary classification of cancel culture, but rather as a spectrum. If an ad hoc swarm becomes larger and larger, the attention from media towards the cancel culture candidate increases correspondingly. As soon as the cancel culture case has a sufficient attention (i.e. the ad hoc swarm is of sufficient size), newspapers are going to pick it up as cancel culture. As soon as this happens, an amplification loop begins where more and more people start searching the web regarding this cancel culture case, which on the other hand pushes the news even further in the most popular queries ranking. If the case becomes big enough, the given target will correlate with the key word "cancel culture" on Google Trends for the given time period. Previous work has shown that Google Trends can be used as a reliable source to measure the interest in conservation topics and the role of online news within the internet (Nghiem et al., 2016), especially also for exploring cancel culture (Etheve, 2020). We are going to pick up on these insights by crawling through short time periods on Google Trends and investigating search terms (cancel culture candidates) that correlate to "cancel culture".

3.2. Collection Procedure

The cancel culture cases are collected as follows:

1. find candidates on Google Trends (e.g. using the Google Trends API)
2. check in newspapers if cancel culture case
3. identify first occurrence of cancel culture case
4. gather cancel culture case from Twitter (before and after)

Once a cancel culture candidate "entity" is found on Google Trends, news articles from that time referencing that entity are investigated. For this, we use Google's advanced search, that allow us to query news articles in the corresponding time window of the gathered tweets. If this entity is canceled according to §2.1, the candidate is added to the corpus. This step is essential, as an entity can be associated with cancel culture just by speaking out on the subject.
Following up, the found articles are explored to determine the first date of the cancel culture case. To be able to analyze the data, tweets mentioning the target entity are scraped before and after the first occurrence of cancel culture.

3.3. Shortcomings of Data Collection

The proposed data collection technique requires a lot of manual work, which is very time-consuming. Furthermore, the cancel culture cases investigated are on top of the cancel culture spectrum, i.e. the ones which got the most global attention.

4. Feature Generation

We use the following features: various output probabilities from pre-trained language models that capture the affective state (which we will describe in 4.1) and action features in the form of verb frequency and tweet frequency (which we will further explore in 4.2). Verb frequency aims to estimate cancel action and tweet frequency aims to estimate the ad hoc swarm size. Respectively, a time interval T is introduced that corresponds to some cancel culture case D. This cancel culture case has $D_t \subset D$ that contains all tweets of one day t. The generated features f for a time interval t are all part of the feature vector F_t. For this feature vector, many models are combined to support the modelling process that we will explore further. Measuring the size of ad hoc swarm is done by counting

[1] https://github.com/Justus-Jonas/Cancel-Culture-Corpus

the number of tweets per t and then normalizing them over the observed time span T. This normalized tweet frequency for the corresponding time span t is added to the feature vector F_t.

4.1. Text Classification

The text classification approach is based onsec an existing RoBERTa models from TweetEval tweeteval, which are used for five tweet classification tasks. The following models with the corresponding features are included:

- Sentiment analysis with *positive, neutral and negative*
- Offensive language detection with *offensive*
- Hate speech detection with *hate*
- Irony detection with *irony*
- Emotion detection with *anger, joy, sadness and optimism*

Before the data are fed into the model, non-textual noise is removed (like links, images, etc.). For every tweet of a day t in the time interval T, all Softmax Scores outputs per tweet F_s of the models are generated, which are then averaged for each day. This gives a set of sentiment and classification features (F_{s_t} for each day, as equation 1 shows.

$$\forall f \in F_s, t \in T : \overline{f_t} = \frac{\sum_{d \in D_t} f_t(d)}{|D_t|} \quad (1)$$

Finally, the aggregated outputs of each day are used as features for the mathematical framework. Due to the size of tweets processed, the number of investigated tweets is limited per day to 10000 for computational reasons.

4.2. Action Analysis

In order to be able to measure the frequency of cancel culture as described in §2.3.3, all cases are scraped with 10 days prior to the initial cancel culture event. The data are split into two, prior cancel culture and during cancel culture. Both data sets are preprocessed, in which we remove non-textual noise and apply lemmatization. To identify verbs, Part-of-Speech tagging is applied. Following, the frequency of every verb is calculated over all cancel culture cases (with its prior cancel culture data). Now, the frequencies of the two vectors V_C (verb frequency cancel culture) and V_B (verb frequency before cancel culture) are subtracted from each other $V = V_C - V_B$. The most frequent verbs are added to the cancel culture verb dictionary.

Applying Action Analysis

With the generated cancel culture verb dictionary, terms are counted for every time step t and are aggregated together to form a continuous value. Similar to the tweet frequency (`frequency_normalized`), this continuous value is $0 - max$ normalized (`verb_freq_normalized`) and both are given as an additional feature as F_A in the modelling process. These features are concatenated with F_s to one feature vector F.

5. Data Analysis

As part of the data analysis, investigated the generated feature vector F of 22 manually identified cancel culture cases. Overall, all cases follow a similar pattern with little variation. In the following we will describe general characteristics of cancel culture and special cases we observed. Nonetheless, we provide a more detailed analysis in the appendix C in table 1 where we investigate the Pearson correlation between the tweet frequency (the size of the ad hoc swarm) and other features.

5.1. Tweet Frequency

As shown in the first sub-figure (left) of figure 1 Jimmy Fallon got canceled on day 7. While the negative sentiment increases rapidly, the most obvious increase in the total number of tweets, which is linked to the size of the ad hoc swarm. This behavior generalizes to most observed cancel culture cases, but might differ in its extremes. An observed cancel culture case from `@Pepsi` multiplied tweets by a factor of around 53 within two days while in the case of Jimmy Fallon only a factor of about 15 is observed. In cases where the attention before was very low (`@Shanemgillis`) where we observed jumps from 27 tweets a day to over 120000 tweets a day. While we did not run in any problems of extreme fluctuations of Sentiment values due to the small number of tweets before the cancel event, this still might be something to keep in mind when working on cancel culture cases where an entity usually does not retrieve as much public attention.

Nonetheless, we also found some special cases (see appendix `@gabecake`) where we observe a significant raise in frequency prior to the actual cancel culture event. After investigating Gabi DeMartino related news articles on the 11/30/2020, one day before the corresponding Twitter account `@gabecake` got canceled, we found that she launched a new product and teased a new song that gave her a lot of positive public attention on that day [2]. One day after that she posted a video on a platform which got her banned for ethical and legal concerns [3] and caused the phenomena of cancel culture. We investigated two similar cases where either the dynamic of the public opinion changed due to new events happening in a debate `@UnburntWitch` [4] or where a large supportive movement emerged simul-

[2] https://www.justjaredjr.com/2020/11/30/gabi-demartino-launches-new-fragrance-beautiful-mess

[3] https://www.buzzfeednews.com/article/tanyachen/onlyfans-suspended-youtuber-gabi-demartinos-

[4] https://bentcorner.com/zoe-quinn-alec-holowka-suicide/

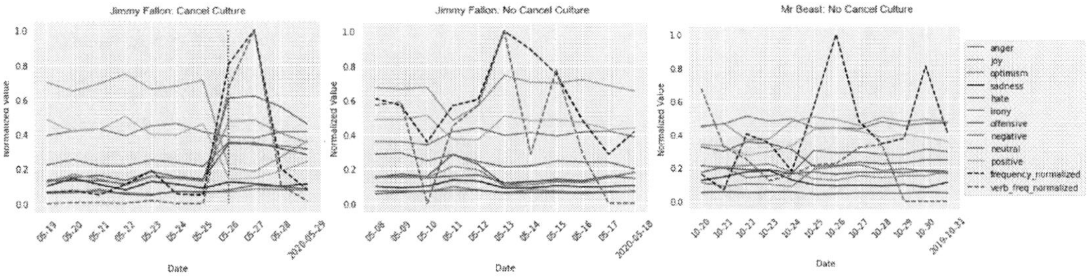

Figure 1: A case of cancel culture (05-19-2020 - 05-29-2020) vs a non cancel culture (05-08-2020 - 05-18-2020) vs. an anti cancel culture event Mr. Beast (10-20-2019 - 10-31-2019)

taneously `@Lin_Manuel` [5] [6]. The pearson correlation coefficients between negative Sentiment values and frequency reflect on that (see Appendix C).

5.2. Cancel Culture associated Verbs Frequency and Text Classification

Apart from the increase of negative and decrease of positive sentiment, the normalized frequency of cancel culture associated verbs strongly correlates with a cancel culture event, while it randomly fluctuates in cases of non cancel culture as it can be seen in subfigure (middle) of figure 1. This dataset is also of Jimmy Fallon, ten days before the figure on the left begins (prior to the cancel culture event). The third graph shows an "anti" cancel culture case when Mr Beast, a famous YouTuber, started Team Trees, an initiative to plant a lot of trees, which got him a great amount of positive attention. Demonstrating that the standalone feature of tweet frequency is not sufficient for identification of cancel culture. One such a feature that helps to distinguish cancel culture is anger. As can be seen in the first graph, anger increases on the day that Jimmy Fallon is canceled. Similar can be observed for negativity, offensive language, irony and the negated for joy and positivity.

The first graph shows an interesting characteristic of cancel culture. After Jimmy got canceled for about 2 days, the frequency of tweets about him dropped drastically, indicating that people lost interest in actively tweeting about him. However, the amount of anger and negativity lingers after the amount of tweets drops. Further exploration shows that this phenomenon generalizes to most other cancel culture cases. The average duration of the spike in frequency, which is calculated by the difference between the day with the highest increase in frequency and the day with the largest decrease in frequency, is only 1.95 until it approaches its baseline again. The same is calculated for the spike in negative sensitivity, and there the average duration is 2.95. From the gathered data, it can therefore be concluded that the negativity in general stays longer than the increase in attention.

[5] https://mickeyblog.com/2020/07/05/review-hamilton-is-the-best-movie-of-2020

[6] https://edition.cnn.com/2020/07/07/entertainment/lin-manuel-miranda-hamilton-slavery/index.html

6. Mathematical Framework for identifying Cancel Culture

As described in §3.2, investigating news articles is necessary to identify whether cancel culture is present in a particular case. This section presents a technique that automatically identifies cancel culture and therefore allows a complete automation of the proposed gathering process introduced in §3. We define a mathematical framework based on the data analysis of §5. The complete model is split up into two phases, as shown in Figure 2. First, a model is used to determine whether cancel culture is present in the given dataset or not. If cancel culture is present, a different statistical model detects on which day the target got canceled exactly.

6.1. Cancel Culture Identification

In order to detect whether cancel culture is present in the dataset, the features that are generated by the Text Classification and the action analysis are aggregated per day. Additionally, the normalized frequency of tweets is added as an additional feature. Now that the features are aggregated, the model adds all scores of negative emotions
$F_n = \{\text{anger, sadness, hate, irony, offensive, negative}\}$
together, aggregated by day, which gives a 'negativity score'. Then, the day with the highest negativity score is compared to the day with the lowest negativity score before t occurred to calculate the slope. The difference between the feature values F_D, calculated in equation 4 of those two days specified in Equations 2 & 3 is then used as a feature vector for a cancel culture dataset D to detect cancel culture.

$$F_{D_{max}} = \max_{t \in T}\left(\sum_{f \in F_{n_t}} f\right) \tag{2}$$

$$F_{D_{min}} = \min_{t' \in \{0,..,t_{max}-1\}}\left(\sum_{f \in F_{n_{t'}}} f\right) \tag{3}$$

$$F_D = F_{D_{\max}} - F_{D_{min}} \tag{4}$$

Once the final features F_D are generated, a Support Vector Machine (SVM) classification model is used to test our hypothesis whether Cancel Culture on Twitter can be identified. The SVM uses an RBF kernel with

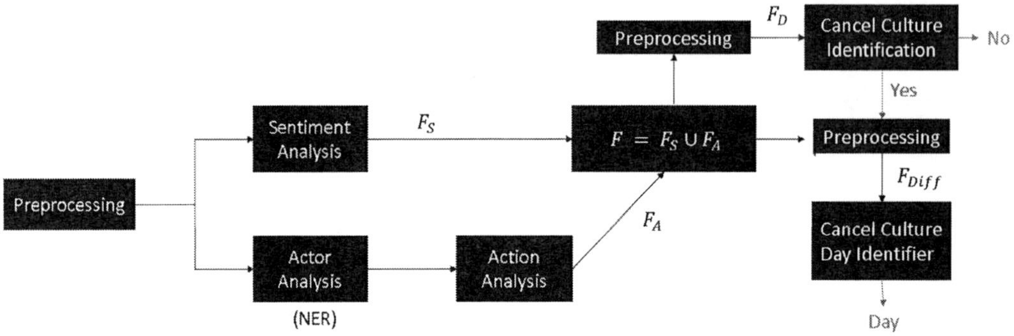

Figure 2: From Feature Generation to the General Model containing the Cancel Culture Identification and Cancel Culture Day Identifier.

a regularization parameter of 2 to be able to create a decision boundary, where all data points on one side of the decision boundary indicate an absence of cancel culture, and all data points on the other side of the decision boundary indicate a presence of cancel culture.

6.2. Cancel Culture Day Identification

In order to detect the date on which the target was canceled, a date identifier algorithm is used after a cancel culture case is predicted. In particular, the difference between every feature for each day is computed so the value of increase or decrease respectively can be distinguished. Furthermore, the day that cancel culture case has occurred is selected according to the maximum negative increase of activity. In other words, the day that has the highest negative change on the calculated difference of the features is declared to be the day that cancel culture occurred. Finally, a delta time value is calculated, which is the difference between the sum of the largest changes and the value of the first day, in order to distinguish the deviation. Below, the mathematical formula 5 shows how the difference is calculated, while equation 6 shows the process on finding the biggest slope of negative increase F_{Diff} using the negative features F_n for a time step t with $F_{Diff_{n_t}}$.

$$F_{Diff} = F_t - F_{t-1} \tag{5}$$

$$t_{start} = \max_{t \in T}\Big(\sum_{f \in F_{Diff_{n_t}}} f\Big) \tag{6}$$

t_{start} is then selected as the first day of cancel culture.

6.3. Evaluation Results

To test our hypothesis of the provided framework, the 20 cancel culture cases are mixed with 23 negative events, of which 20 are prior cancel culture data of the corresponding cases (the week before the cancel culture event) and 3 "anti" cancel culture cases like Mr. Beast (see §5) that demonstrate an adhoc swarm. The model is able, apart from one data point, to separate all cases from each other. For the Cancel Culture Day Identifier, the standard deviation is calculated for the amount of days the statistical model is off on its prediction. On the current dataset, the day identification model has an average deviation 0.59 days. We also have used this model to enlarge the data set. Specifically, we gathered 4 more cases (2 positive and 2 negative) of which the model was able to identify cancel culture correctly. The two positive cases (`Bob Baffert` and `pepe le pew` have been added to the data set while the negative samples (`Katt Williams` and `Rowan Atkinson`) have been added to the appendix B. Based on news article investigations, we could confirm that the identified starting days t_{start} were in both positive cases correct.

6.3.1. Permutation Feature Importance

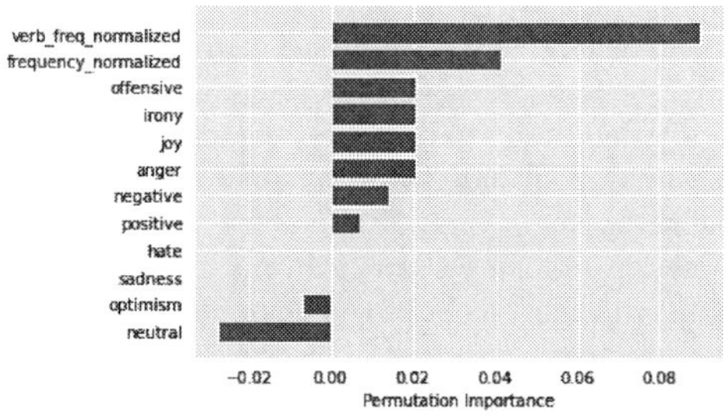

Figure 3: Permutation Feature Importance of identifying cancel culture

To get an idea of the importance of each feature, the SVM is given the same data set as a classification task, where the permutation feature importance is measured. As figure 3 demonstrates, the normalized verb frequency is most important, which aligns with the hypothesis stated in §5. Furthermore, frequency plays a significant role in detecting a cancel culture event. Offensiveness, joy, anger, irony, followed by negativity are the most important sentimental and emotional features, which also aligns with the hypothesis in §5. While the hate language detection model has already shown in the data analysis 1 that it seems not to correlate with cancel culture, similar to the positive score, we interpret this insignificance due to the redundancy of other correlating features. The assumptions in §5 of the irrelevance of sadness and optimism amplified.

7. Discussion

Concluding from §6.3.1, the sufficient elements to identify cancel culture appear to be a combination of sentiment analysis, emotion detection and irony detection (of tweeteval) together with the frequency of tweets (i.e. a measurement for the size of the ad hoc swarm) and the presence of verbs that correlate with cancel culture (action analysis).

7.1. Limitations

While both models seem to be able to create decision boundaries that make the feature vectors of cancel culture and non cancel culture events separable, it is important to note that as described in §3.3 the gathered data is biased by the attention from the media like news organizations. Entities of public interest are therefore more likely to be picked up by our gathering technique, which is why our findings are only representative to cases of public figures.

While we had some cases like Goya (see §C) where the baseline prior was only a few tweets a day, this might get even worse when looking at more privately preserved cases. This could easily lead to fluctuations in the frequencies as well as text classification values, leading to a misclassification due to the way that the values per day are aggregated, a day with a very small amount of tweets can easily become an outlier. For example, if on a certain day only two people tweet about them and both of these tweets are negative, this can create a spike in negativity that might trick the model into believing that the target gets canceled on that day, especially if on the other days the number of tweets was even lower.

Moreover, we addressed the problem of dynamic changes within public opinion that might change very quickly or create movements that happen simultaneously, making the identification more difficult (see §5 for `@gabecake` etc.). Considering the Cancel Culture Day Identifier, one limitation is that the fact that the only consideration is the increase of features per day. However, if a person starts getting canceled at the end of the day, this increase might not be apparent immediately, and it will only become visible on the next day. In order to circumvent this, the data could be split per hour instead of per day. A downside to this is that more data would be needed, this is especially a problem if only a few number of tweets per day are given as baseline.

7.2. Research Questions

Given the previous analysis, we can conclude that cancel culture can be identified with the limitation to public figures, answering our first research question. Similarly, as far as RQ2 is concerned, we have demonstrated that using Google Trends as well as the provided mathematical framework can be used for automatically expanding the data set.

8. Conclusion

This paper introduces cancel culture to the computational literature and demonstrates that it's a phenomenon that can be empirically observed and studied using a combination of NLP techniques, including sentiment analysis and emotion detection. We find that cancel culture is rather short-lived, with an attention peak of 1.95 days and a peak in negative expression of 2.95 days (§5). Furthermore, we introduce a first public data set with over 2.3 million tweets of 22 cancel culture cases and a mathematical framework for automatically enlarging it in the future. Gathering such large number of tweets is very time-consuming, not only because of API constraints but also considering that every single tweet has to be processed by 5 different Transformer models. We hope that with a joint call to the interdisciplinary social medial analysis community, we can scale up this data set together to get more insight in this new emerging social phenomenon.

References

Bender, E. M. and Friedman, B. (2018). Data statements for natural language processing: Toward mitigating system bias and enabling better science. *Transactions of the Association for Computational Linguistics*, 6:587–604.

Bouvier, G. and Machin, D. (2021). What gets lost in twitter 'cancel culture' hashtags? calling out racists reveals some limitations of social justice campaigns. *Discourse & Society*, 32(3):307–327.

Cantrell, K. and Bickle, S. (2021). Cat in a spat: scrapping Dr Seuss books is not cancel culture.

Carr, N. K. (2020). How Can We End #cancelculture - Tort Liability or Thumper's Rule? *The Catholic University Journal of Law and Technology*, 28:15.

Chiou, R. (2020). We need deeper understanding about the neurocognitive mechanisms of moral righteousness in an era of online vigilantism and cancel culture. *AJOB Neuroscience*, 11(4):297–299. PMID: 33196355.

Clark, M. D. (2020). Drag them: A brief etymology of so-called "cancel culture". *Communication and the Public*, 5(3-4):88–92.

Etheve, S. (2020). Exploring cancel culture.

Gerstmann, E. (2020). Cancel Culture Is Only Getting Worse.

Helmore, E. (2021). 'It's a moral decision': Dr Seuss books are being 'recalled' not cancelled, expert says, March.

Hine, G. E., Onaolapo, J., De Cristofaro, E., Kourtellis, N., Leontiadis, I., Samaras, R., Stringhini, G., and Blackburn, J. (2017). Kek, Cucks, and God Emperor Trump: A Measurement Study of 4chan's Politically Incorrect Forum and Its Effects on the Web. *arXiv:1610.03452 [physics]*, October. arXiv: 1610.03452.

Hooks, A. M. (2020). Cancel culture: Posthuman hauntologies in digital rhetoric and the latent values of virtual community networks. page 107.

Kato, B. (2020). What is cancel culture? Everything to know about the toxic online trend, July.

Mishan, L. (2020). The long and tortured history of cancel culture, Dec.

Ng, E. (2020). No grand pronouncements here...: Reflections on cancel culture and digital media participation. *Television & New Media*, 21(6):621–627.

Nghiem, L. T. P., Papworth, S. K., Lim, F. K. S., and Carrasco, L. R. (2016). Analysis of the capacity of google trends to measure interest in conservation topics and the role of online news. *PLoS ONE*, 11.

Provost, C. (2020). 'Cuties' culture war is dramatic and global – but no surprise.

Randall, M. E. (2021). Cancel culture and the threat to progress in radiation oncology. *Practical Radiation Oncology*.

Romano, A. (2019). Why we can't stop fighting about cancel culture, Dec.

Shen, W. (2017). Online Privacy and Online Speech: The Problem of the Human Flesh Search Engine. *University of Pennsylvania Asian Law Review*, 12:44.

Thomas, Z. (2020). What is the cost of 'cancel culture'? *BBC News*, October.

Veil, S. R. and Waymer, D. (2021). Crisis narrative and the paradox of erasure: Making room for dialectic tension in a cancel culture. *Public Relations Review*, 47(3):102046.

Velasco, J. C. (2020). You are cancelled: Virtual collective consciousness and the emergence of cancel culture as ideological purging. *Rupkatha Journal on Interdisciplinary Studies in Humanities*, 12(5).

Zurcher, A. (2021). Cancel culture: Have any two words become more weaponised? *BBC News*, February.

A. A special case of Cancel Culture

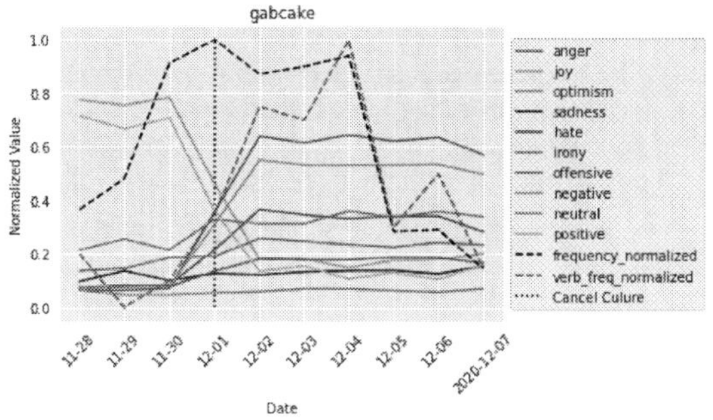

Figure 4: gabcake cancel culture case showing a significant increase in frequency right before cancel culture event.

B. Data Gathering: Negative Samples

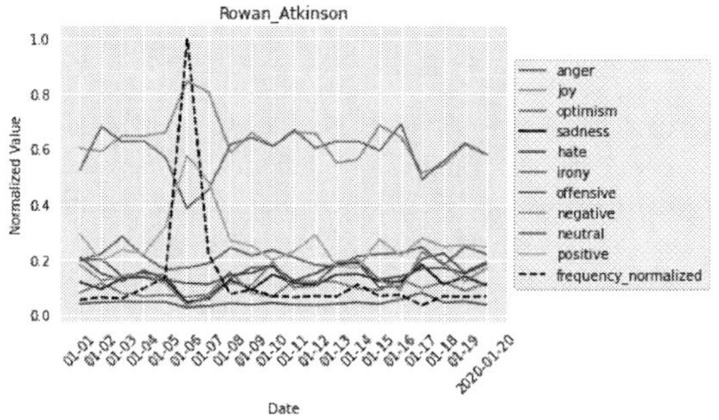

Figure 5: Rowan Atkinson talked about cancel culture which led to a Google trends correlation

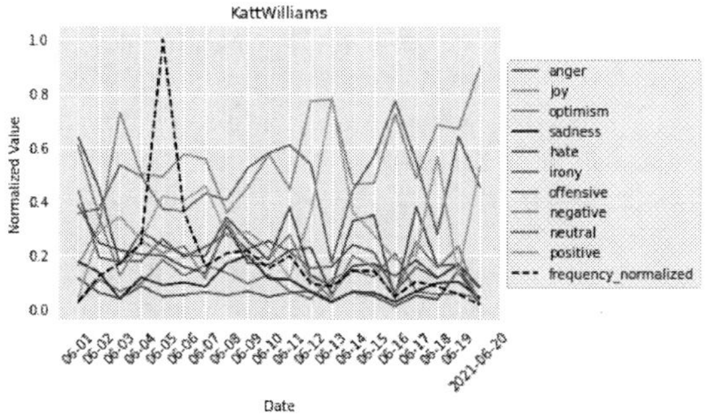

Figure 6: Katt Williams talked about cancel culture which led to a Google trends correlation

C. Analysis Cancel Culture Cases

Table 1: Every Cancel Culture Case (in order) by name, number of total tweets, min number of tweets per day, max number of tweets per day, first day of gathered data, last day of gathered day, the identified first day of cancel culture and the Pearson correlation coefficients between the frequency (the size of the ad hoc swarm) and the other features.

Name	number tweets	min tweets	max tweets	first date	last date	cancel date	Pearson correlation coefficients to frequency of Tweets										
							anger	joy	sadness	optimism	irony	hateful	offensive	positive	neutral	negative	verb freq
Lin_Manuel	173423	3025	57053	7/1/20	7/12/20	7/4/20	-0.37	0.33	0.08	-0.43	0.14	-0.32	-0.23	0.63	-0.83	-0.31	0.94
UnburntWitch	5214	10	2192	8/24/19	9/6/19	8/31/19	-0.5	-0.23	0.77	0.64	-0.19	-0.55	-0.37	0.43	-0.46	-0.18	0.86
alisoneroman	21756	59	14844	5/6/20	5/15/20	5/8/20	0.39	-0.36	-0.1	-0.02	0.26	0.55	0.42	-0.41	-0.13	0.44	1.0
armiehammer	7374	41	1797	1/8/21	1/17/21	1/10/21	0.47	-0.41	-0.51	0.27	0.5	0.15	0.69	-0.67	0.57	0.65	0.86
bobbaffert	2595	22	869	5/7/21	5/17/21	5/9/21	0.58	-0.49	0.14	-0.37	0.62	0.53	0.61	-0.47	-0.58	0.62	0.9
CarsonKing2	8777	34	4745	9/16/19	9/29/19	9/25/19	0.6	-0.67	0.43	-0.11	0.18	-0.14	0.36	-0.62	0.38	0.55	1.0
dojacat	185425	3978	49731	5/21/20	5/30/20	5/22/20	0.41	-0.58	0.85	-0.7	0.59	-0.38	0.67	-0.62	-0.43	0.62	0.98
gabcake	11657	276	1881	11/28/20	12/7/20	12/1/20	-0.02	0.04	-0.28	-0.2	0.12	-0.04	0.04	0.04	-0.06	-0.03	0.5
ginacarano	264909	849	121959	2/8/21	2/17/21	2/10/21	0.5	-0.53	-0.28	-0.29	0.61	-0.11	0.44	-0.46	-0.16	0.55	1.0
goya	228223	1461	108553	7/6/20	7/13/20	7/9/20	0.6	-0.6	-0.13	0.57	0.63	0.48	0.56	0.63	-0.65	0.57	1.0
jamescharles	132301	2503	32749	5/7/19	5/16/19	5/10/19	0.28	-0.28	0.53	-0.22	0.59	0.25	0.36	-0.39	0.37	0.39	0.98
jimmyfallon	46476	884	18108	5/19/20	5/28/20	5/26/20	0.86	-0.86	0.23	0.18	0.84	0.6	0.87	-0.83	-0.71	0.88	0.96
jk_rowling	89803	1147	28968	9/9/20	9/18/20	9/13/20	0.62	-0.61	0.53	-0.47	0.72	-0.06	0.85	-0.8	-0.36	0.69	0.99
LanaDReyOnline	349450	10374	152633	5/16/20	5/25/20	5/21/20	0.74	-0.74	0.68	-0.52	0.62	0.63	0.75	-0.68	-0.65	0.69	1.0
MorganWallen	59051	846	19968	2/1/21	2/9/21	2/3/21	0.68	-0.69	0.67	-0.32	0.46	0.1	0.73	-0.67	-0.87	0.77	0.99
pepe le pew	42960	36	10775	3/1/21	3/14/21	3/6/21	0.56	-0.61	0.4	0.11	0.4	-0.69	0.45	-0.72	-0.1	0.41	0.82
pepsi	298336	2679	156846	3/30/17	4/8/17	4/4/17	0.75	-0.7	0.33	-0.12	0.7	0.16	0.7	-0.69	-0.7	0.73	1.0
projared	71702	27	40000	5/6/19	5/15/19	5/9/19	0.45	-0.42	0.04	-0.43	0.48	0.52	0.58	-0.39	-0.6	0.55	0.97
sebastian stan	4609	146	1897	7/9/20	7/18/20	7/14/20	0.83	-0.82	0.7	-0.72	0.63	0.28	0.8	-0.77	-0.5	0.84	0.99
seuss	167600	383	43424	2/15/21	3/6/21	2/27/21	0.79	-0.79	0.38	-0.71	0.76	0.48	0.78	-0.74	-0.38	0.76	0.98
Shanemgillis	50889	6	16193	9/10/19	9/20/19	9/12/19	0.53	-0.55	0.49	0.15	0.31	0.24	0.52	-0.5	-0.49	0.59	0.95
starbucks	165210	7454	49505	6/6/20	6/15/20	6/10/20	0.91	-0.92	-0.12	0.13	0.8	0.59	0.89	-0.92	-0.92	0.94	0.96

Proceedings of LATERAISSE Workshop @LREC2022, pages 26–31
Marseille, 25 June 2022
© European Language Resources Association (ELRA), licensed under CC-BY-NC-4.0

Benchmarking Language Models for Cyberbullying Identification and Classification from Social-media texts

Kanishk Verma[a], Tijana Milosevic[b], Keith Cortis[c], Brian Davis[d]
ADAPT SFI Research Centre, Dublin City University[a-d]
DCU Anti Bullying Centre [a-b]
Dublin, Ireland
{kanishk.verma, keith.cortis, brian.davis}@adaptcentre.ie
tijana.milosevic@dcu.ie

Abstract

Cyberbullying is bullying perpetrated via the medium of modern communication technologies like social media networks and gaming platforms. Unfortunately, most existing datasets focusing on cyberbullying detection or classification are i) limited in number ii) usually targeted to one specific online social networking (OSN) platform, or iii) often contain low-quality annotations. In this study, we fine-tune and benchmark state of the art neural transformers for the binary classification of cyberbullying in social media texts, which is of high value to Natural Language Processing (NLP) researchers and computational social scientists. Furthermore, this work represents the first step toward building neural language models for cross OSN platform cyberbullying classification to make them as OSN platform agnostic as possible.

Keywords: Benchmarking, Cyberbullying, Cross-platform, Classification, Transformers

1. Introduction

The *cyberbullying* nomenclature and its propagation medium has evolved over the years, but it can still be understood as a hostile and aggressive behaviour to intentionally and repeatedly hurt or embarrass someone over the internet. Cyberbullying has only exacerbated over recent months due to the COVID-19 pandemic, which has resulted in a surge in online activity among young people. (McBride, 2021), (Raisbeck, 2020), (Jain et al., 2020). Victims of such an act of bullying propagated over the internet may experience lower self-esteem, increased suicidal ideation, and mixed negative emotional responses. (Hinduja and Patchin, 2014).

Recent studies by (Chen and Li, 2020) (Salawu et al., 2020) have leveraged deep neural network (DNN) and neural language modelling (LM) approaches like **B**idirectional **E**ncoder **R**epresentations for **T**ransformers (BERT) by (Devlin et al., 2018) to model cyberbullying detection and classification. As studied by (Emmery et al., 2021), many previous studies in this field of cyberbullying detection are bound by scanty datasets from specific OSN platforms. .

This study aims to develop a cyberbullying text classification language model by evaluating it across multiple Online Social Networking (OSN) platforms to achieve an OSN agnostic cyberbullying classification language model. To that end, we conduct experiments to benchmark pre-trained language models - BERT by (Devlin et al., 2018) and HateBERT by (Caselli et al., 2020) on real-life cyberbullying textual datasets. Although our intent is to cover all OSN platforms, due to the limited nature of the existing research, we are only able to leverage **390,934** sentences or phrases from real-life cyberbullying textual datasets provided by (Hosseinmardi et al., 2015), (Rafiq et al., 2015), (Xu et al., 2012), (Salawu et al., 2020), and (Van Hee et al., 2018). We also establish baselines using traditional Machine Learning (ML) algorithms to benchmark the neural language models.

2. Related Work

Most of the current work in this field by (Tomkins et al., 2018),(Van Hee et al., 2018) ,(Talpur BA, 2020) is focused on social-context-based approaches for binary classification of cyberbullying texts, and these studies rely on Word2Vec by (Goldberg and Levy, 2014), Glove by (Pennington et al., 2014), and FastText (AI, 2015) based word representation techniques. Despite the satisfactory results of recent studies with an amalgamation of NLP and DNN techniques, studies by (Van Hee et al., 2018), (Samghabadi et al., 2020), (Emmery et al., 2019) are bound to ASK.fm data. Studies (Salawu et al., 2020), (Tahmasbi and Rastegari, 2018), (Chatzakou et al., 2017) are restricted to only Twitter data, and studies by (Chen and Li, 2020), (Sourodip Ghosh, 2020), (Paul, 2020) take a multimodal approach, i.e., text supplemented by social network analysis (SNA)[1] features, are bound to only Instagram and Vine datasets published by (Hosseinmardi et al., 2015) and (Rafiq et al., 2016) respectively.

Other studies by (Sprugnoli et al., 2018), (Bretschneider and Peters, 2016) and a dataset published by (Van Hee et al., 2018) have participant-level annotations that help identify roles of cyberbullying like *harasser, bystander or victim*. Given that the scope of this study focuses on the binary classification of cyberbullying texts, these datasets are not explored for multi-class

[1]SNA: The process of investigating social structures through the use of networks and graph theory

cyberbullying classification, and labels of the dataset by (Van Hee et al., 2018) are converted to binary form, i.e., *bullying* or *non-bullying*.
Also, studies by (Rafiq et al., 2016), (Noviantho et al., 2017), (Al-Ajlan and Ykhlef, 2018), (Hamiza Wan Ali et al., 2018) in cyberbullying text classification have used the traditional ML algorithm Support Vector Machines (SVM) (Wang et al., 2006), as a ML baseline and some other studies by (Dadvar and Eckert, 2018), (Paul, 2020), (Sourodip Ghosh, 2020) have used Bi-directional Long Short-Term Memory (Bi-LSTM) (Huang et al., 2015) for language modelling. To that effect, this study makes the following key contributions,

- First steps to benchmark transformer-based models, neural network and machine learning models for binary classification of cyberbullying texts sourced from real-life cyberbullying textual datasets.
- First steps towards developing an OSN agnostic cyberbullying detection model by training language models on text from one type of OSN platform and evaluating it across multiple OSN platform-types.

3. Experimental Setup

3.1. Datasets

Instagram (IG)[2] dataset sourced from (Hosseinmardi et al., 2015), Vine[3] dataset sourced from (Rafiq et al., 2015), hereafter referred to as *User-Comment datasets* (UC), are similar multimedia content sharing platforms, as they allow users to comment, like and share, multi-media content with one another. ASK.fm[4] and Formspring.me (F.me)[5] datasets sourced from (Van Hee et al., 2018), hereafter referred to as *Question-Answering datasets* (QA) are an anonymous question and answering social networking platform. Twitter[6] datasets sourced from (Xu et al., 2012) and (Salawu et al., 2020), hereafter referred as *Twitter datasets*, are from the OSN platform, Twitter - that allows users to share 280 characters of text as messages termed *tweets*. The lenghts of tokens (words) in each phrase or comment within each of the *seven* dataset, depicts the platform similarity, as represented in the Figure 1. This helps understand that similar platforms have almost similar lengths of tokens. The label and sentence-level details is depicted in Table 1. Each merged dataset is split into 70% for training, 20% for validation, and the remaining 10% is held out for test-set. All language models trained on the three merged datasets were evaluated individually across the 10% hold-out test for all merged datasets.

Dataset	Platforms	# of Sentences	Bullying %
User - Comments (UC)	IG + Vine	249,123	23.53%
Question - Answering (QA)	Ask.fm + F.me	129,501	4.60%
Twitter	Twitter	12,310	6.51

Table 1: Percentage-wise Bullying Label Distribution and Sentence Count of all datasets

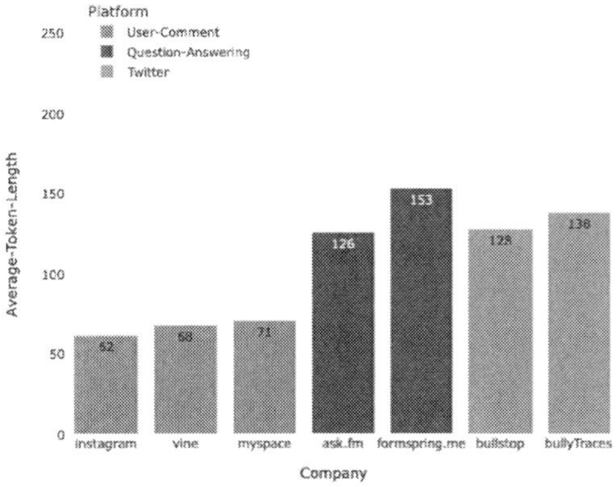

Figure 1: Average lengths of tokens in datasets

3.2. Data Imbalance

There is a high imbalance skewed toward the non-bullying class in all datasets, as depicted in Figure 2. Handling the imbalance is paramount to avoid any learning bias towards the majority class. As the dataset is limited in bullying instances, to avoid any risk of contextual loss and not to alter the sequence of words in sentences, we ruled out the synthetic minority oversampling technique (SMOTE) (Chawla et al., 2002) and the random under-sampling technique (Prusa et al., 2015). Instead, we leveraged the random over-sampling technique (Fernández et al., 2018), i.e., a technique that duplicates examples of minority class randomly, to balance the data towards the majority class.

3.3. Data Pre-processing

Adhering to General Data Protection Regulation (GDPR) directive (Council of European Union, 2016), we fully anonymised and normalised the datasets for any PII[7] data by leveraging GATE Cloud (Tablan et al.,

[2] https://about.instagram.com/
[3] https://en.wikipedia.org/wiki/Vine_(service)
[4] https://ask.fm/
[5] https://en.wikipedia.org/wiki/Spring.me
[6] https://about.twitter.com/en

[7] Refers to Personally identifiable information

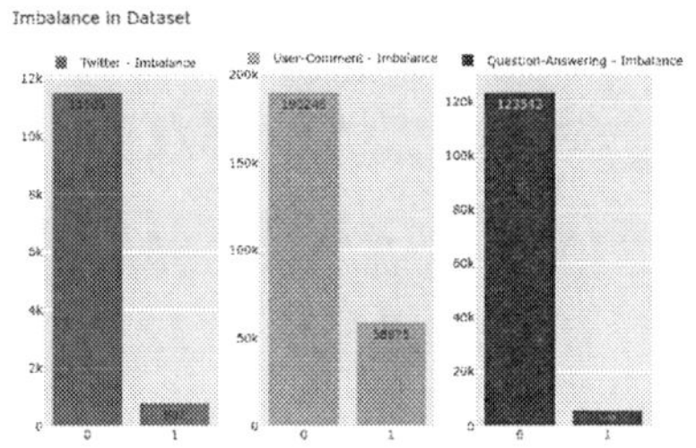

Figure 2: Imbalance in Dataset

2013). Furthermore, the TwitIE API (K. Bontcheva, 2013) to extract named entities in the text. In addition, we also a) removed URLs, user mentions, and non-ASCII characters for all datasets, b) retweet (RT) markers in text for *twitter* datasets, c) lower-cased all text, and d) converted textual contractions to formal format.

3.4. Language Models

Each neural classifier is fine-tuned by adding a fully connected layer on top of its respective pre-trained model.

- **BERT**: Provided by (Devlin et al., 2018), with 12 layers, also known as *transformer blocks*, and trained with 110 M parameters. We fine-tune pre-trained $BERT_{base-uncased}$ language model with different hyperparamters. (See Section 3.5).

- **HateBERT**: Provided by (Caselli et al., 2020), it is a re-trained $BERT_{base-uncased}$ language model, trained on comments from RAL-E Reddit's banned communities[8]. Further pre-training of BERT model is an effective and cost ineffective strategy to port pre-trained language model for other language specific tasks.

- **Bi-LSTM**: A baseline deep neural network model based on Bi-directional Long Short-Term Memory (Huang et al., 2015). We trained this model on five epochs with different hyper-parameters and pre-trained 50 dimensional GloVe-based Twitter word-embedding.

- **Support Vector Machines (SVM)**: A traditional machine learning algorithm known as Support Vector Machines proposed by (Hearst et al., 1998). This algorithm is trained by leveraging Term Frequency - Inverse Document Frequency (TF-IDF) (Zhang et al., 2011).

[8] `https://en.wikipedia.org/wiki/Controversial_Reddit_communities`

3.5. Hyper-parameters and evaluation

- **Hate-BERT** & **BERT**: Our experiments[9], utilised the implementations provided by HuggingFace's Transformer library (Wolf et al., 2019) and the authors of HateBERT. We used the *ModelForSequenceClassifcation* which matches BERT model to the proper implementation. We trained the transformer-based models for `2,3,4` epochs and fine-tuned each model for all 3 merged datasets individually and thus the maximum sequence length varied between `128` to `256` tokens depending on the dataset. We fine-tuned the classification layer for transformer-based models using *ReLU* and the *Adam Weighted* optimizer by (Kingma and Ba, 2015) with a learning rate ranging from `0.1`, `0.001`, $1e^{-5}$ to $5e^{-5}$.

- **Bi-LSTM**: For the Bi-LSTM model, the recurrent dropout rate was set to 0.2 and the fully connected layer was added with 256 neurons and *ReLU* activation function, and since it was engineered for a binary task, the output layer was set to *softmax*. The *Cross Entropy loss* function was used for fine-tuning both transformer-based models and training Bi-LSTM.

- **SVM**: For the SVM model, we first conducted a grid search with five cross-validation and the hyper-parameters from the best model were used for training.

To benchmark and evaluate the fine-tuned transformer-based models, we conducted experiments with one traditional approach using SVM with TF-IDF and one Bi-LSTM algorithm with GloVe-based pre-trained 50-dimensional vectors. In addition, we evaluate the performance of these language models based on F1 scores (Chinchor and Sundheim, 1993) for positive (bullying) and negative (non-bullying) and overall F1 scores. F1 scores consider both the precision and recall to compute their metrics, and it can be interpreted as the weighted average of the two classes.

4. Results

As indicated in Table 2, the fine-tuned Hate-BERT language model has a significant advantage over the fine-tuned BERT, Bi-LSTM and traditional SVM. Although our experiment results indicated in the Table 2 show that models trained and tested on texts from the same OSN platform perform better when evaluated across different OSN platforms. The Hate-BERT language model, when fine-tuned on the *Question-Answering* datasets (ASK.fm and Formspring.me) and *Twitter* datasets for binary classification of cyberbullying text, has outperformed other baselines earlier discussed in the Section 3.4. Although the SVM model

[9] All the experiments in this work were conducted on a local system with a 16 core CPU, 16GB RAM and a NVIDIA RTX 2070 GPU (8GB GPU Memory)

trained on *user-comment* datasets (Myspace, Vine, Instagram) performs well with a **0.75** F1 score in classifying bullying samples as bullying, the same model only performs with **0.56** F1-score for classifying bullying samples. The Bi-LSTM model trained on *Twitter* datasets performs well with a **0.69** F1-score for classifying bullying samples, the same model achieves **0.63** F1-score for classifying bullying samples for the *user-comment* dataset. Additionally, our experiments depict that when the Hate-BERT model is fine-tuned on the *Question-Answering* datasets, it is able to achieve **0.73** F1-score in classifying bullying samples for both *user-comment* and *question-answering* dataset. Moreover, when we fine-tune the Hate-BERT model on *twitter* datasets, though it achieves **0.78** F1-score for *twitter* datasets, it is only able to achieve **0.71** F1-score for classifying bullying samples for the *user-comment* dataset. These exhaustive experiments indicate that fine-tuning language models from three OSN platforms are the first step toward developing an OSN platform-agnostic cyberbullying detection mechanism. Moreover, our results suggest that more work will be beneficial in developing such platform-agnostic detection mechanisms.

5. Conclusion & Future Work

We have provided a comprehensive benchmark on the binary classification of cyberbullying in a social media text. Our experiments demonstrate that merging existing datasets from similar platforms can improve the performance of transformer-based models. Also, fine-tuning the pre-trained Hate-BERT model outperforms the BERT, Bi-LSTM and SVM models. This novel benchmarking study is the first step toward building an OSN agnostic neural language model for the cyberbullying domain. One limitation of our study is that we use word-count (TF-IDF) and non-contextual word-embeddings (Glove) for text representation while training the baseline models - SVM and Bi-LSTM. Instead, future research should leverage contextual word embeddings from BERT and Hate-BERT language models for training these baseline models. The current availability of datasets and resources in the area of cyberbullying, as highlighted by (Emmery et al., 2021) and observed in this study, is scarce and highly skewed to negative class, i.e., to non-bullying instances. Therefore, there is a need to divulge qualitative and not quantitative cyberbullying research to build better language models to detect cyberbullying. Moreover, a detailed ablation study of the language models will aid in future benchmarking of such cyberbullying classifiers. In addition, it will help clarify how language models better classify specific samples from certain classes than the others.

Model	**Train-set**	**Test-set**	**Bully F-1**	**Non-bully F1**	**Avg F1**
SVM	UC	UC	**0.75**	0.71	**0.73**
		QA	**0.56**	0.58	**0.57**
		Twitter	0.51	0.51	0.51
	QA	UC	0.34	0.50	0.42
		QA	0.52	0.54	0.53
		Twitter	0.52	0.52	0.52
	Twitter	UC	0.28	0.50	0.39
		QA	0.48	0.50	0.49
		Twitter	0.54	0.54	0.54
Bi-LSTM	UC	UC	0.68	0.70	0.69
		QA	0.30	0.50	0.40
		Twitter	0.51	0.51	0.51
	QA	UC	0.58	0.60	0.59
		QA	0.69	0.67	0.68
		Twitter	0.52	0.54	0.53
	Twitter	UC	**0.63**	0.61	**0.62**
		QA	0.61	0.57	0.59
		Twitter	**0.69**	0.67	**0.68**
BERT	UC	UC	0.65	0.77	0.71
		QA	0.54	0.58	0.56
		Twitter	0.58	0.60	0.59
	QA	UC	0.48	0.50	0.49
		QA	0.62	0.68	0.65
		Twitter	0.57	0.61	0.59
	Twitter	UC	**0.54**	0.52	**0.53**
		QA	0.63	0.61	0.62
		Twitter	**0.75**	0.79	**0.77**
Hate-BERT	UC	UC	**0.68**	**0.84**	**0.76**
		QA	0.67	0.59	0.63
		Twitter	**0.65**	0.71	**0.68**
	QA	UC	**0.73**	0.65	**0.69**
		QA	**0.73**	0.73	**0.73**
		Twitter	0.61	0.65	0.63
	Twitter	UC	**0.71**	0.65	**0.68**
		QA	0.69	0.65	0.67
		Twitter	**0.78**	0.84	**0.81**

Table 2: All Results

6. Acknowledgements

We would like to thank the authors (Hosseinmardi et al., 2015), (Rafiq et al., 2015), (Van Hee et al., 2018), (Xu et al., 2012), (Salawu et al., 2020) for sharing the data.

This research has received funding from the *Irish Research Council* and *Google* under grant number EP-SPG/2021/161, *Facebook/Meta Content Policy Award*, Phase 2: Co-designing with children: A rights-based approach to fighting bullying. In addition, this research has also received funding from the European Union's Horizon 2020 research and innovation programme under the Marie Skłodowska-Curie grant agreement No. 801522, by Science Foundation Ireland and co-funded by the European Regional Development Fund through the ADAPT Centre for Digital Content Technology grant number 13/RC/2106_P2.

7. Bibliographical References

AI, F. (2015). Fasttext. https://ai.facebook.com/tools/fasttext/, November. Facebook AI.

Al-Ajlan, M. A. and Ykhlef, M. (2018). Optimized twitter cyberbullying detection based on deep learning. In *2018 21st Saudi Computer Society National Computer Conference (NCC)*, pages 1–5.

Bretschneider, U. and Peters, R. (2016). Detecting cyberbullying in online communities.

Caselli, T., Basile, V., Mitrovic, J., and Granitzer, M. (2020). Hatebert: Retraining BERT for abusive language detection in english. *CoRR*, abs/2010.12472.

Chatzakou, D., Kourtellis, N., Blackburn, J., Cristofaro, E. D., Stringhini, G., and Vakali, A. (2017). Mean birds: Detecting aggression and bullying on twitter. *CoRR*, abs/1702.06877.

Chawla, N. V., Bowyer, K. W., Hall, L. O., and Kegelmeyer, W. P. (2002). Smote: synthetic minority over-sampling technique. *Journal of artificial intelligence research*, 16:321–357.

Chen, H.-Y. and Li, C.-T. (2020). Henin: Learning heterogeneous neural interaction networks for explainable cyberbullying detection on social media. *arXiv preprint arXiv:2010.04576*.

Chinchor, N. and Sundheim, B. M. (1993). Muc-5 evaluation metrics. In *Fifth Message Understanding Conference (MUC-5): Proceedings of a Conference Held in Baltimore, Maryland, August 25-27, 1993*.

Council of European Union. (2016). Regulation (eu) 2016/679 of the european parliament and of the council (general data protection regulation). https://eur-lex.europa.eu/eli/reg/2016/679/oj.

Dadvar, M. and Eckert, K. (2018). Cyberbullying detection in social networks using deep learning based models; A reproducibility study. *CoRR*, abs/1812.08046.

Devlin, J., Chang, M.-W., Lee, K., and Toutanova, K. (2018). Bert: Pre-training of deep bidirectional transformers for language understanding. *arXiv preprint arXiv:1810.04805*.

Emmery, C., Verhoeven, B., Pauw, G. D., Jacobs, G., Hee, C. V., Lefever, E., Desmet, B., Hoste, V., and Daelemans, W. (2019). Current limitations in cyberbullying detection: on evaluation criteria, reproducibility, and data scarcity. *CoRR*, abs/1910.11922.

Emmery, C., Verhoeven, B., De Pauw, G., Jacobs, G., Van Hee, C., Lefever, E., Desmet, B., Hoste, V., and Daelemans, W. (2021). Current limitations in cyberbullying detection: On evaluation criteria, reproducibility, and data scarcity. *Language Resources and Evaluation*, 55(3):597–633.

Fernández, A., García, S., Galar, M., Prati, R. C., Krawczyk, B., and Herrera, F. (2018). *Learning from imbalanced data sets*, volume 10. Springer.

Goldberg, Y. and Levy, O. (2014). word2vec explained: deriving mikolov et al.'s negative-sampling word-embedding method. *CoRR*, abs/1402.3722.

Hamiza Wan Ali, W. N., Mohd, M., and Fauzi, F. (2018). Cyberbullying detection: An overview. In *2018 Cyber Resilience Conference (CRC)*, pages 1–3.

Hearst, M., Dumais, S., Osuna, E., Platt, J., and Scholkopf, B. (1998). Support vector machines. *IEEE Intelligent Systems and their Applications*, 13(4):18–28.

Hinduja, S. and Patchin, J. W. (2014). *Bullying beyond the schoolyard: Preventing and responding to cyberbullying*. Corwin press.

Hosseinmardi, H., Mattson, S. A., Rafiq, R. I., Han, R., Lv, Q., and Mishra, S. (2015). Analyzing labeled cyberbullying incidents on the instagram social network. In *International conference on social informatics*, pages 49–66. Springer.

Huang, Z., Xu, W., and Yu, K. (2015). Bidirectional LSTM-CRF models for sequence tagging. *CoRR*, abs/1508.01991.

Jain, O., Gupta, M., Satam, S., and Panda, S. (2020). Has the covid-19 pandemic affected the susceptibility to cyberbullying in india? *Computers in Human Behavior Reports*, 2:100029.

K. Bontcheva, L. Derczynski, A. F. M. G. D. M. N. A. (2013). witie: An open-source information extraction pipeline for microblog text. *Proceedings of the International Conference on Recent Advances in Natural Language Processing*.

Kingma, D. P. and Ba, J. (2015). Adam: A method for stochastic optimization. In Yoshua Bengio et al., editors, *3rd International Conference on Learning Representations, ICLR 2015, San Diego, CA, USA, May 7-9, 2015, Conference Track Proceedings*.

McBride, M. (2021). Cyberbullying soared during lockdown. what are schools doing about it? https://www.irishtimes.com/news/education/cyberbullying-soared-during-lockdown-what-are-schools-doing-about-it-1.4473011, Feb. The Irish Times.

Noviantho, Isa, S. M., and Ashianti, L. (2017). Cyberbullying classification using text mining. In *2017 1st International Conference on Informatics and Computational Sciences (ICICoS)*, pages 241–246.

Paul, S., S. S. (2020). Cyberbert: Bert for cyberbullying identification. *Multimedia Systems*.

Pennington, J., Socher, R., and Manning, C. D. (2014). Glove: Global vectors for word representation. In *Proceedings of the 2014 conference on empirical methods in natural language processing (EMNLP)*, pages 1532–1543.

Prusa, J., Khoshgoftaar, T. M., Dittman, D. J., and Napolitano, A. (2015). Using random undersampling to alleviate class imbalance on tweet sentiment data. In *2015 IEEE International Conference on Information Reuse and Integration*, pages 197–202.

Rafiq, R. I., Hosseinmardi, H., Han, R., Lv, Q., Mishra,

S., and Mattson, S. A. (2015). Careful what you share in six seconds: Detecting cyberbullying instances in vine. In *2015 IEEE/ACM International Conference on Advances in Social Networks Analysis and Mining (ASONAM)*, pages 617–622. IEEE.

Rafiq, R. I., Hosseinmardi, H., Mattson, S. A., Han, R., Lv, Q., and Mishra, S. (2016). Analysis and detection of labeled cyberbullying instances in vine, a video-based social network. *Social network analysis and mining*, 6(1):1–16.

Raisbeck, D. (2020). Experts around the world warn parents to be vigilant as cyberbullying increases during lockdown. `https://www.cybersmile.org/news/experts-around-the-world-warn-parents-to-be-vigilant-as-cyberbullying-increases-during-lockdown`. The Cybersmile Foundation.

Salawu, S., He, Y., and Lumsden, J. (2020). Bullstop: A mobile app for cyberbullying prevention. In *Proceedings of the 28th International Conference on Computational Linguistics: System Demonstrations*, pages 70–74.

Samghabadi, N. S., Monroy, A. P. L., and Solorio, T. (2020). Detecting early signs of cyberbullying in social media. In *Proceedings of the Second Workshop on Trolling, Aggression and Cyberbullying*, pages 144–149.

Sourodip Ghosh, Aunkit Chaki, A. K. (2020). Cyberbully detection using 1d-cnn and lstm. *Proceedings of International Conference on Communication, Circuits and Systems*.

Sprugnoli, R., Menini, S., Tonelli, S., Oncini, F., and Piras, E. (2018). Creating a WhatsApp dataset to study pre-teen cyberbullying. In *Proceedings of the 2nd Workshop on Abusive Language Online (ALW2)*, pages 51–59, Brussels, Belgium, October. Association for Computational Linguistics.

Tablan, V., Roberts, I., Cunningham, H., and Bontcheva, K. (2013). Gatecloud.net: a platform for large-scale, open-source text processing on the cloud. *Philosophical Transactions of the Royal Society A: Mathematical, Physical and Engineering Sciences*, 371(1983):20120071.

Tahmasbi, N. and Rastegari, E. (2018). A socio-contextual approach in automated detection of public cyberbullying on twitter. *Trans. Soc. Comput.*, 1(4), December.

Talpur BA, O. D. (2020). Cyberbullying severity detection: A machine learning approach.

Tomkins, S., Getoor, L., Chen, Y., and Zhang, Y. (2018). A socio-linguistic model for cyberbullying detection. In *2018 IEEE/ACM International Conference on Advances in Social Networks Analysis and Mining (ASONAM)*, pages 53–60.

Van Hee, C., Jacobs, G., Emmery, C., Desmet, B., Lefever, E., Verhoeven, B., De Pauw, G., Daelemans, W., and Hoste, V. (2018). Automatic detection of cyberbullying in social media text. *PloS one*, 13(10):e0203794.

Wang, Z.-q., Sun, X., Zhang, D.-x., and Li, X. (2006). An optimal svm-based text classification algorithm. In *2006 International Conference on Machine Learning and Cybernetics*, pages 1378–1381.

Wolf, T., Debut, L., Sanh, V., Chaumond, J., Delangue, C., Moi, A., Cistac, P., Rault, T., Louf, R., Funtowicz, M., and Brew, J. (2019). Huggingface's transformers: State-of-the-art natural language processing. *CoRR*, abs/1910.03771.

Xu, J.-M., Jun, K.-S., Zhu, X., and Bellmore, A. (2012). Learning from bullying traces in social media. In *Proceedings of the 2012 conference of the North American chapter of the association for computational linguistics: Human language technologies*, pages 656–666.

Zhang, W., Yoshida, T., and Tang, X. (2011). A comparative study of tf*idf, lsi and multi-words for text classification. *Expert Systems with Applications*, 38(3):2758–2765.

Proceedings of LATERAISSE Workshop @LREC2022, pages 32–41
Marseille, 25 June 2022
© European Language Resources Association (ELRA), licensed under CC-BY-NC-4.0

Identifying Hate Speech using Neural Networks and Discourse Analysis Techniques

Zehra Melce Hüsünbeyi, Didar Akar, Arzucan Özgür
Department of Computer Engineering, Department of Linguistics, Department of Computer Engineering
Bogaziçi University
melce.husunbeyi@gmail.com, akar@boun.edu.tr, arzucan.ozgur@boun.edu.tr

Abstract

Discriminatory language, in particular hate speech, is a global problem posing a grave threat to democracy and human rights. Yet, it is not always easy to identify, as it is rarely explicit. In order to detect hate speech, we developed Hierarchical Attention Network (HAN) based and Bidirectional Encoder Representations from Transformer (BERT) based deep learning models to capture the changing discursive cues and understand the context around the discourse. In addition, we designed linguistic features using critical discourse analysis techniques and integrated them to the these neural network models. We studied the compatibility of our model with the hate speech detection problem by comparing it with traditional machine learning models, as well as a Convolution Neural Network (CNN) based model, a Convolutional Neural Network-Gated Recurrent Unit (CNN-GRU) based model which reached significant performance results for hate speech detection. Our results on a manually annotated corpus of print media in Turkish show that the proposed approach is effective for hate speech detection. We believe that the feature sets created for the Turkish language will encourage new studies in the quantitative analysis of hate speech.

Keywords: deep learning, hierarchical attention network, bert, linguistic features

1. Introduction

Hate speech is defined by the European Council as "any statement including racist hate, ethnocentrism [...] religion intolerance against minorities, immigrants or originally-immigrant groups [...] and any expressions spreading, provoking or legitimating hate." [1] Hate speech has grown exponentially and become more visible around the world as various social media platforms and conventional media become more accessible to people. Turkey is no exception in this regard. Given the potential harm hate speech can cause in terms of human rights, social justice and democracy, it is not surprising that both national and international institutions and large-scale businesses are interested in monitoring this phenomenon. The protocol signed by Council of Europe and Facebook, Microsoft, Twitter, and YouTube in 2016 to detect illegal hate speech can be given as an example of this monitoring attempt (Jourová, 2016). The protocol has been later extended to cover more platforms such as Instagram, Google+, Snapchat, and Dailymotion in 2018.

The first step in the fight against hate speech is obviously to detect it. Manual detection of hate speech which has been the common practice in many institutions requires an enormous amount of time, effort and work force, and therefore, is not sustainable. Instead, automating the identification process would be highly advantageous. However, detection and defining discourse is not an easy task due to the dynamic and contextual nature of language. The same sentence or text can mean different things when used by different speakers belonging to different social groups or when uttered in different contexts. Even if we can define the context, irony and implicit or implied meanings can still create serious problems for detecting hate speech. Therefore, it is essential to find ways of examining various clues about discourse and its context.

This study is partially based on a master's thesis by (Hüsünbeyi, 2020). In the thesis, a model has been developed for the automatic detection of hate speech through the HAN (Yang et al., 2016), which aims to detect changes in the meaning by using the hierarchical structure of texts. Then task specific linguistic features were used to enhance this neural network model and the results showed that these novel linguistic methods were effective in distinguishing news texts with hate speech from the ones without it. These linguistics features include certain forms of othering language such as possessive pronouns and lexical choices indicating the subjectivity level of the news texts. To the best of our knowledge, this is the first study that utilizes manually annotated data for hate speech in the print media of Turkey and we believe it will promote new studies with the potential of gathering different agents and disciplines. Later on, in order to further improve the results we got for the thesis, we have also considered Transformer-based BERT(Devlin et al., 2019) model, which offers the latest state-of-the-art solutions to numerous NLP problems. We investigated whether the BERT model, which processes long sequences limited by input length constraint and does not use the knowledge of the hierarchical structure of documents, unlike the HAN model, would enhance the performance of

[1] Recommendation No. R (97) 20 of the Committee of Ministers to member states on "hate speech"

our task. We took into consideration BERTurk[2], pre-trained language model for Turkish, and examined how it would yield results with the proposed architecture and novel linguistic features.

2. Related Work

In the detection of hate speech, domain specific and traditional linguistic features have a significant role. There are some commonly used features in the literature (Xu et al., 2012; Gitari et al., 2015; Burnap and Williams, 2016a) such as part of speech tags (POS), typed dependency relations. As one of the most promising linguistic approaches, the othering language concept was utilized as a framework to determine hate speech for contents on social media (Burnap and Williams, 2016b; Alorainy et al., 2019). By using the Stanford Lexical Parser (De Marneffe et al., 2006). (Burnap and Williams, 2016b) presented syntactic grammatical relationships in a tweet to obtain opposition. For example, the typed dependency relation nsubj(home, them) in the "send them back home" sentence identifies the relational sense between the tokens and underlines the divergence between 'us' and 'them'. They also stated that statistically significantly better results were achieved with the othering feature set, especially for detecting hate speech related to religious beliefs. According to (Alorainy et al., 2019), othering language theory, based on the combination of linguistics approaches such as set of in group (us) / out group (they) separation in hate speech samples that include 'two-sided' pronoun (us vs them).

Besides linguistics related features, surface features e.g., n-grams, bag-of-words (BOW), local features e.g., TF-IDF weights of tokens, and rule-based approaches e.g., errors in spelling, and the count of punctuation marks were used with traditional machine learning algorithms. According to the recent survey in (Mishra et al., 2019), the most commonly used model in the detection of hate speech systems is Support Vector Machines (SVM), and other commonly utilized learning algorithms are Random Forests, Decision Trees, and Naive Bayes.

In recent times, deep learning-based approaches such as Convolutional Neural Networks (CNNs), Recurrent Neural Networks (RNNs), word and paragraph embeddings have been successfully used in Natural Language Processing (NLP) problems. (Badjatiya et al., 2017) developed CNN and LSTM neural network models with random embeddings or GloVe embeddings using a dataset which contains 16K annotated tweets labeled as 'sexist', 'racist', and 'neither sexist nor racist' (Waseem and Hovy, 2016). These task specific learned embedding weights have also been used as features along with SVM and Gradient Boosting Decision Tree (GBDT) classifiers. The best evaluation score was obtained by tuning random embeddings with LSTM and then by using these weights to train a GBDT classifier. Character and word-level CNN have also been used in several works. The combination of these models achieves higher performance than a character n-gram Logistic Regression model as reported by (Park and Fung, 2017). In order to obtain long range dependencies on social media data, (Zhang et al., 2018; Wang, 2018) considered combining CNN and RNN sequentially. (Zhang et al., 2018; Wang, 2018). More recently, transformer based approaches such as the BERT model (Devlin et al., 2019) and its variants have gained importance with their power of learning large language models. The effectiveness of these models have also been demonstrated in the recent hate speech detection shared tasks at Semeval-2019 (Liu et al., 2019), Semeval-2020 (Wiedemann et al., 2020), and HASOC-2020 (Mishraa et al., 2020).

While deep learning models often do not contain manually designed linguistic features, it has become important to use linguistics to get a better idea of how the model works and to avoid generalization errors. We integrate and examine the contribution of hate speech signaling linguistic structures to the HAN model. We focus on hate speech detection in the Turkish language, which is a morphologically rich and agglutinative language. At the Semeval-2020 task, a Turkish Track was organized and a Twitter dataset which is an extended version of the dataset studied by (Çöltekin, 2020), was provided to the participants. The first two ranked teams utilized multi-lingual pre-trained Transformers based on XLM-RoBERTa (Wang et al., 2020) and ensemble of CNN-LSTM, BiLSTM-Attention, and BERT models as well as word embeddings (Ozdemir and Yeniterzi, 2020). To the best of our knowledge, there is only one prior study on the automatic detection of hate speech in Turkish news articles (Coban and Filatova, 2019), where traditional machine learning models with automatically annotated data were used. In this paper, we use manually annotated data from print media and develop a novel hybrid approach for Turkish hate speech detection by integrating linguistic features with a deep learning model.

3. Methodology

3.1. Dataset

In this study, we used a dataset of print media news articles, the manual annotations of which were obtained from Hrant Dink Foundation, who have been monitoring the media for hate speech since 2009 in the scope of the Media Watch Project (Hrant Dink Foundation, 2021). Within the scope of this project, the foundation monitors all national and approximately 500 local newspapers in Turkey methodically through the media monitoring company 'PRNet'. The news articles including a predetermined set of 'keywords' are examined along with the critical discourse analysis methods and annotations are made manually based on Recommendation No. R(97) 20 of the Committee of Ministers of the Council of Europe.

[2]https://huggingface.co/dbmdz/bert-base-turkish-cased

The dataset that we obtained from the foundation consists of 18316 annotated news articles published between 2016-2018, with two classes: 9309 news articles not containing hate speech and 9007 news articles containing hate speech. Both classes are composed of news articles that contain prominent words regarding ethnic or religious identity, which makes the task of distinguishing articles with hate speech from the ones without hate speech more challenging. This dataset, which was scanned by OCR, is quite noisy. It contains non-Turkish character strings and distorted news texts. To enhance the performance of the developed models, we lower-cased all tokens, and removed the non-Turkish characters and numbers as well as the URL links. Then, we divided the dataset into 60% train, 20% validation, and 20% test splits for model development.

3.2. Linguistic Processing of Hate-Speech

We developed several linguistic features taking into account the qualitative analysis of hate discourse in the Turkish language. The novel methods to generate task-specific features are examined in this section.

3.2.1. Othering Language

The opposition between 'we' and 'you' is typically used in biased texts, while 'we' has positive representations, and 'you' or sometimes 'they' receive negative representation. This opposition can lead to discrimination and hate speech by reinforcing blaming and mockery directed at 'you' (Oktar and Değer, 1999; Oktar, 2001).

In order to detect the opposition between the positive representation of "we" and the negative representation of "you", we made use of some discursively constrained morpho-syntactic properties of Turkish that are listed below. To this end, we got part-of- speech (POS) tags and typed dependencies in the sentences by using Universal Dependencies Pipe (UDPipe) (Straka and Straková, 2017) with the UD Turkish Treebank (IMST-UD) model (Sulubacak et al., 2016).

1. Turkish is a pro-drop language; in other words subject pronouns can be dropped because verbs are inflected with obligatory person agreement morphemes. When a subject pronoun is not dropped, it serves discourse functions such as contrastive focus and foregrounding person information. Based on this feature we extracted sentences with overt subject pronouns in first person conjoined with sentences with overt subject pronouns in second person.
2. Another case of opposition can be established when the subject of the first sentence is used as a complement in the following sentence.
3. The genitive construction in Turkish also follows the pro-drop principle. Since the noun is obligatorily inflected with the possessive agreement marker, the pronoun marking the possessor can be dropped. When the genitive pronoun is overtly present, it is also used for contrastive focus or foregrounding purposes. Based on this feature, we extracted sentences containing genitive pronouns followed by nouns marked with possessive person agreement (-Im, -ImIz, -In, -InIz, -(s)I).

In the training set, we found that hate-speech labeled news indeed include sentences with the 'othering language' features described above.

- The following extract from the dataset it can be seen that the use of overt subject pronouns sets up oppositions between biz 'we' and siz 'you'.
  '*Biz her daim bu millet ile savaşan güçler olduğunu bilerek yaşıyoruz. Düşmanlarımızın olduğunu, onların bu mücadeleyi asla bırakmayacağını bilerek yaşıyoruz! Siz ise ne tarihi göz önüne alıyor, ne zamane şartlarını göz önüne alıyor, ne de zerre kadar vicdan gösteriyorsunuz!. Biz devletimize güveniyoruz! Her ne olursa olsun devletimizin yanındayız, yanında olacağız! Biz bu toprakları vatan yapmak için yüzyıllardır can veririz, can alırız! [...]*'[3]
  'We are always aware of the existence of some forces against our nation. We are always aware of our enemies, who won't give up. Yet, you don't care about the history, conditions of today or a bit conscience. We trust in our state! No matter what happens, we stand by our state, and we will continue to do so! We have been dying and killing for centuries in order to make these lands our homeland!'
- The following extract illustrates the use of overt genitive pronouns to set up oppositions between 'you' and 'us' followed by an overt subject pronoun in second person with the same effect.
  [...] Yani kendi ülkemizdeki sizin uşağınız Haçlı zihniyeti ile mücadele ettik. Bu bizim utancımız değil. Ama sizin büyük bir utancınız var. Almanlar, yani sizler Hitler gibi korkunç bir katili yarattınız. Ülkenizin sokaklarında hala gamalı haçlı Nazi artıkları dolaşıyor. İnsanları sabun fabrikalarında yakan bir Nazi despotu sizin eserinizdir. Genetiğinizde soykırımcılık var. Siz onların torunlarısınız. [...], '[...] In other words, we struggled with your servant Crusader mentality in our own country. This is not our shame. But you have a great shame. You, the Germans, created a terrible killer like Hitler. Nazi scraps with swastikas still roam the streets of your country. A Nazi despot who burns people in soap factories is your achievement. You have genocidalism in your genetics. You are their descendants.[...]'

[3]Right after each Turkish text shown in Italic, we provide its English translation

3.2.2. Use of Imperatives

In media texts, imperative structures are occasionally used and like the aforementioned structures, they, too, represent the opposition between "we" and "you" (Oktar and Değer, 1999). Imperative structures in these oppositional contexts typically display the authority and power of "we" over "you", because imperative sentences imply that the language user has the power to give orders (Kress and Hodge, 1997).

We have utilized UDPipe to obtain imperative morphemes on the verbs. For example, *"Gavur gavurluğunu bil edebinle otur."* 'Infidel, know your infidelity and know your place.' has been parsed 'otur' has been identified as imperative verb_root. Here the word infidel is associated with non-Muslims and it is a derogatory term. It functions as a political tool targeting 'Western' and European countries. In this sentence the addressee (i.e. the infidel) is ordered to know their place and behave accordingly. Imperative expressions as in this example emphasize power, authority and consequently the superiority of 'us' on 'you'.

3.2.3. Reported Speech Forms

In general, subjective media language tends to include hate discourse (Çınar, 2013). To detect objectivity/subjectivity we have considered reported speech, in particular reporting verbs. A list of 30 reporting verbs has been created to detect texts covering reported speech. Some of these tokens reflect objectivity in the news language such as açıklamak 'explain', dile getirmek 'state', and aktarmak 'report', while others include the interpretation of the journalist such as suçlamak 'accuse' and iddia etmek 'to claim'. The changing narrative with the usage of reported speech form can be observed in a sample sentence from the dataset; *'Gavur gazeteleri kin kusmaya devam ediyor. Türkiye düşmanlarının hevesleri kursaklarında kalınca hazımsızlıkları gazetelerine de yansıdı. Gavur İngiltere'nin Independent gazetesi Orta Doğu muhabiri Cockburn, işgal girişimi sonrası hainlerin açığa alınmasının Türkiye'yi zayıflattığını iddia etti.'*, 'Infidel newspapers continue to throw up hatred. When the enemies of Turkey couldn't get what they wanted, their indigestion reflected on their newspapers. Infidel Cockburn, the Middle East correspondent of Britain's Independent newspaper, claimed that the suspension of traitors after the invasion attempt weakened Turkey.'

3.2.4. Encoding of Linguistic Features

The linguistic patterns described in Section 3.2 have been used to constitute novel linguistic feature sets for our task. We developed two separate feature sets. *ling_set1* captures the othering language and use of imperatives rules. If a news article includes these linguistic patterns, the portion of the document consisting of the sentences containing these patterns is extracted and used as *ling_set1*. Otherwise, if the news article doesn't includes any of these linguistic patterns, *ling_set1* consists of the entire document itself.

Our second feature set, *ling_set2* holds the information of the existence of reported speech expressions, which were encoded using the one-hot encoding scheme. In addition, three numerical features are calculated for each document, namely the ratio of sentences containing othering language, the ratio of sentences containing imperative language, and the ratio of sentences containing reported speech forms. These three dimensional numerical feature vectors are concatenated to the one-hot encoded vectors of reported speech expressions to form *ling_set2*.

Document embedding with *ling_set1*

It has been shown that the embedding representations of documents with similar semantics of context belong to a related part of space (Le and Mikolov, 2014). Considering that previous studies obtained effective results (Nobata et al., 2016; Alorainy et al., 2019) in the detection of hate speech by using document embeddings, which provide the semantics of texts to be captured, we have created document embedding for our problem. *Ling_set1* and documents not including patterns have been processed along with The Distributed Memory Model of Paragraph Vectors (PV-DM) (Le and Mikolov, 2014) to obtain low dimensional vectors of the documents with vector size = 300, window size = 5, and number of training epochs = 30.

3.3. Proposed Deep Learning Models

Hate speech reflected in the national and local press, unlike social media texts, is implicit and representative. While the explicit hate speech language often contains sexist or racial slur words, they are usually not applied in implicit media language. Abusive language is disguised by vague terms, ridicule, profanity, and other means, rather than using explicit language. As Van Dijk pointed out, discourse that controls semantic markers, such as media, can only be considered along with its context (Van Dijk, 2011). HAN and BERT based models have been implemented to address the contexts and changing meanings of words and sentences in different texts.

3.3.1. HAN for Hate-speech Detection

HAN (Yang et al., 2016) uses knowledge of the hierarchical structure of texts. The architecture of the model consists of word encoder, word attention, sentence encoder and sentence attention layers. Words of delivered sentence have been embedded and relevant context of each sentence which is called annotations of words have been extracted through Bidirectional GRU (Bahdanau et al., 2014). To emphasize connotation words for representing sentence meaning, word annotation layer gets output of encoder layer and produces a sentence vector with indicative words. Likewise the word level calculations, document vector has been obtained by feeding the sentence vector to the network.

We implemented the HAN model based on (Yang et al., 2016) using domain specific word embeddings, which were trained on the training and validation splits of the proposed dataset through fastText (Bojanowski et al., 2017). The hyperparameters were tuned on the validation set as 100 hidden units in the GRU layers, 200 hidden units in the attention layers, and RMSprop optimizer with learning rate 10^{-3}.

HAN with Novel Linguistic Features
As well as obtaining the semantic content of documents with HAN, hate discourse patterns in news articles have been also taken into account to improve our model. For this purpose, *ling_set1* and *ling_set2* have been concatenated to HAN both separately and jointly, and their performance in identifying hate speech was analyzed.
Initially, the pre-trained *ling_set1* were combined HAN model. We processed paragraph vectors through two fully connected layers with 200 and 100 hidden units, respectively, and the Rectified Linear Unit (ReLU) activation function is applied. Before concatenation with document representations, the dropout regularization with a rate of 0.3 was implemented to the attention layer of HAN. The concatenated vectors were fed into a fully connected layer with 200 hidden units through ReLU activation function. Lastly, predictions were generated using the softmax activation function.
In the second case, *ling_set2* were combined HAN model. These external features are concatenated with the output of the attention layer of HAN. We fed the concatenated vectors through a fully connected layer with 200 hidden units and the ReLU activation function. Then, the dropout regularization with a rate of 0.1 was performed to the hidden layer. Finally, the softmax activation function was utilized to create predictions.
In the third case, the pre-trained *ling_set1* as well as *ling_set2* were concatenated. Our proposed architecture was presented in Figure1. Essentially, the previous two models were merged. *ling_set1* and the output of the attention layer with dropout regularization were concatenated and fed to a fully connected layer with 200 hidden units and the ReLU activation function. Then, these document vectors were concatenated to *ling_set2* and processed through a fully connected layer with 200 hidden units and the ReLU activation function. We implemented dropout regularization with a rate of 0.2 to the hidden layer. Lastly, the predictions are created along with the softmax activation function.

3.3.2. BERT for Hate-speech Detection

Transformers based BERT offers a powerful solution for context heavy texts with its structure that bidirectionally examines the incoming text and combines the masked language and next sentence prediction models. The pre-trained Turkish language model, BERTurk with 12 transformers blocks was trained on several Turkish corpora such as the OSCAR corpus[4], a recent Wikipedia dump, and various OPUS corpora[5].

[4]https://oscar-corpus.com/

[5]https://opus.nlpl.eu/

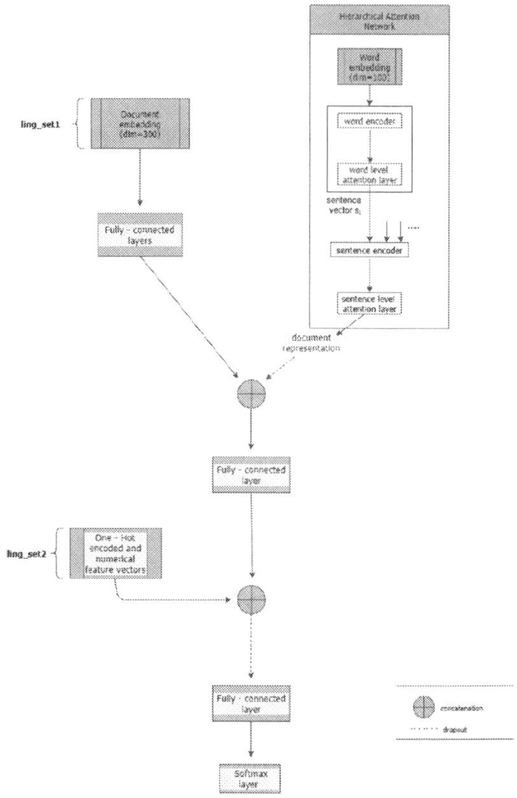

Figure 1: The proposed model incorporates HAN with linguistic features, *ling_set1* and *ling_set2*.

We fine-tuned this uncased BERT model for the detection of hate speech task using the compiled media data. The recommended hyperparameters by (Devlin et al., 2019) were evaluated. Batch-size and common learning rate were chosen as 16 and 5e-5, respectively. Document embeddings were constituted through obtaining the vectors corresponding to the [CLS] token from the final Transformer layer of this fine-tuned BERT model.

BERT embeddings with Novel Linguistic Features
The 768 dimensional feature vector taken from the final transformer layer of BERT model were concatenated with *ling_set1* and *ling_set2*, as similarly in Figure 1. Instead of the output vectors of the attention layer of HAN, vector sequences provided by BERT have been merged with *ling_set1* and passed to a fully connected layer with 200 hidden units and the ReLU activation function. Then, concatenation of *ling_set2* and feature vectors from the previous layers followed same fully connected layer and Dropout regularization steps as in the proposed model. Finally, softmax activation function is performed for obtaining predictions.

4. Experiments and Results

To the best of our knowledge, the only prior work on hate speech detection in Turkish news articles has been conducted by (Coban and Filatova, 2019). They used a data set, where the not-hate speech articles have been sampled from CNN[6] and BBC[7] news under the assumption that they do not include hate-inciting content. We compiled a larger data set, where both hate speech and not-hate speech classes have been manually annotated and evaluated the methods proposed by (Coban and Filatova, 2019), namely SVM with linear kernel, Naive Bayes and Multilayer Perceptron with TF-IDF weighted character and word n-grams, in order to serve as baseline for our proposed linguistically enhanced neural models. In addition, we implemented a Logistic regression classifier and performed a grid search through the validation data set split to get the optimized parameters of the classifiers.

According to our results in Table 1, the overall scores with word n-gram are higher than the ones achieved with char n-grams. Logistic regression obtain the highest scores in all metrics, while the second-highest scores are reached through SVM with linear kernel.

Additionally, the performance of HAN has been compared with CNN and CNN-GRU. It is stated that in the literature, CNN and RNN have been used separately (Le and Mikolov, 2014) and together (Zhang et al., 2018) on social media data and significant performances have been obtained. We have evaluated a CNN model that is based on the model of (Kim, 2014) with 3 parallel convolution layers and kernel sizes of 3, 4, 5 of words with filter size 100 of each for feature extraction. As a state-of-art based model, we have also replicated the CNN-GRU architecture in (Zhang et al., 2018). To maintain consistency, these models have been evaluated on the test set with 3662 documents, 20% of the overall dataset. The word embedding vectors trained via fastText were applied in all deep artificial neural network models. Also, the average evaluation scores with three different fixed seeds and three experimental runs in each fixed seed have been computed for the sake of reliability of the results.

We have observed that HAN outperforms the evaluation scores of traditional ML-based approaches and CNN-based approaches showed in Table 1 and Table 2 in all metrics. Addition of the GRU recurrent layer to the CNN improved the accuracy and macro average f-score with 0.2%. While CNN is good at feature extraction in comparison to the traditional machine learning models, GRU brings the capability of learning sequence dependencies. It can be stated that the attention based HAN model is more compatible with the features of our dataset for the task of hate speech detection. We have compared the performance of HAN with the proposed feature sets. The results in Table 2 show that both *ling_set1* and *ling_set2* enhance the performance of the HAN model and the best results are achieved when the two feature sets are used together.

Our experiments have been extended to BERT which is among the recent state-of-the-art models for hate speech detection and categorization (Wiedemann et al., 2020). Although the BERT constrained with 512 characters long, BERT base model performed better than both HAN base and HAN with linguistic feature sets model. We examined the effect of linguistic features on the BERT model, which significantly affected the performance of the HAN model, as explained in Randomization test section. According to the Table 2, although the linguistic features slightly increased the performance of the BERT model, it is concluded that there is no statistical difference between the two models. (Rogers et al., 2020) stated that BERT embeddings hold especially semantic and syntactical knowledge through multi-head attention layers. Obtained result showed the possibility that the BERT model implicitly capturing the linguistic features which are beneficial for hate speech detection task.

[6]https://www.cnnturk.com/

[7]https://www.bbc.com/turkce

5. Analysis

5.1. Randomization test

We have performed a randomization test (Yeh, 2000), which is widely used in NLP, to examine if there is a significant difference between proposed models. The null hypothesis that *'there is no significant difference between the models'* is rejected when p is less than 0.025 with significance level of alpha = 0.05. With the 9 outcomes from each model, 81 different p-values and their harmonic mean is calculated. With comparison of HAN base and HAN with the linguistic features models, the p-value scores were calculated for hate speech class is 0.007 and the p-value for not hate speech class is 0.008. According to our test statistics the null hypothesis is rejected for both classes. It proves that there is a significant difference between HAN base and HAN with the linguistic features models, suggesting that the novel linguistic features bring further improvement to the HAN model. Another comparison was made between BERT model and BERT with the linguistic features model and the obtained p-value for the hate speech class is 0.188 and for not hate speech class is 0.147. These test statistics state that the null hypothesis is not rejected for both classes and there is no significant difference between these two models.

5.2. Error analysis

Dependency parsing and POS tagging errors affected the feature extraction process and the overall performance. These errors are caused by the parser as well as by OCR.

In addition, we observed that many errors were caused by the incorrect classification of news articles that contain discriminatory language, but not hate speech, as

			accuracy	precision	recall	fscore	fscore macro avg
word (1,2)-gram + tf-idf	SVM	hate_speech	0.857	0.849	0.862	0.856	0.857
		not_hate_speech		0.865	0.852	0.858	
	Logistic Regression	hate_speech	0.864	0.856	0.869	0.862	0.864
		not_hate_speech		0.872	0.858	0.865	
	MultinomialNB	hate_speech	0.810	0.790	0.835	0.812	0.81
		not_hate_speech		0.831	0.785	0.807	
	Multilayer Perceptron	hate_speech	0.834	0.839	0.821	0.830	0.834
		not_hate_speech		0.830	0.847	0.839	
char 2-gram + tf-idf	SVM	hate_speech	0.781	0.771	0.789	0.780	0.781
		not_hate_speech		0.792	0.774	0.783	
	Logistic Regression	hate_speech	0.777	0.768	0.784	0.776	0.777
		not_hate_speech		0.787	0.771	0.779	
	MultinomialNB	hate_speech	0.721	0.741	0.666	0.701	0.720
		not_hate_speech		0.705	0.775	0.739	
	Multilayer Perceptron	hate_speech	0.789	0.764	0.826	0.794	0.789
		not_hate_speech		0.817	0.753	0.784	

Table 1: Evaluation scores for the traditional machine learning based methods

		accuracy	precision	recall	fscore	fscore macro avg
CNN word	hate_speech	0.872	0.862	0.887	0.872	0.872
	not_hate_speech		0.890	0.859	0.872	
CNN + GRU	hate_speech	0.874	0.893	0.849	0.869	0.874
	not_hate_speech		0.864	0.899	0.879	
HAN base	hate_speech	0.889	0.880	0.899	0.888	0.889
	not_hate_speech		0.902	0.879	0.890	
HAN with *ling_set1*	hate_speech	0.895	0.867	0.927	0.898	0.896
	not_hate_speech		0.928	0.861	0.893	
HAN with *ling_set2*	hate_speech	0.893	0.860	0.935	0.896	0.893
	not_hate_speech		0.932	0.853	0.891	
HAN with *ling_set1* + *ling_set2*	hate_speech	0.897	0.883	0.911	0.897	0.897
	not_hate_speech		0.911	0.883	0.897	
BERT	hate_speech	0.904	0.905	0.914	0.906	0.904
	not_hate_speech		0.909	0.894	0.902	
BERT with *ling_set1* + *ling_set2*	hate_speech	0.906	0.901	0.909	0.907	0.906
	not_hate_speech		0.910	0.903	0.904	

Table 2: Evaluation scores of neural network based approaches

belonging to the hate speech class by the classification models, revealing the challenge of distinguishing hate speech from discriminatory language.

6. Conclusion

In this study, a dataset for detection of hate speech in Turkish has been compiled by retrieving 18316 national and local print media news articles. The manual annotations were obtained from the Hrant Dink Foundation, who have been working on manually detecting hate speech in the Turkish media since 2009 and have been releasing annual reports to raise awareness. By utilizing these manually annotated data, a hybrid approach based on deep learning and linguistic features has been developed for Turkish hate speech detection.

Considering the qualitative analysis of hate discourse in the Turkish language, several linguistic features have been designed. The HAN and BERT models were en-

hanced with these novel features and the performance of the new models was analyzed. Our results indicated that the HAN model is able to address the changing interest weights of words based on the context by taking account of the natural segmentation of documents. Better results compared to CNN and CNN-GRU based models have been obtained for hate speech detection using the HAN base model. Combining HAN with pretrained othering and imperative language based features as well as with information about reported speech forms further enhanced the performance. BERT based models have also been fine-tuned for the task of hate speech detection, which achieved the highest performances. The BERT model with the linguistic features closely follows the BERT base model in terms of F-score, and randomization test has shown that there is no significant difference between these two models. It concluded that, BERT model may be implicitly capturing the linguistic features which are beneficial for hate speech detection task. With the developed methods, we aim to minimize dependence on human labor for the identification of hate speech, which is crucial for the elimination of discrimination.
As future work, we are planning to investigate other linguistic properties and what features are most relevant for hate speech detection in the Turkish Language as well as exploring the inductive bias provided by linguistic features with various sizes of the data.

7. Acknowledgements

This research was partially supported by the Swedish Consulate-General, İstanbul Turkey (Project number: UM2021/10687/ISTA). We are also grateful to Hrant Dink Foundation for their collaboration and for sharing their resources which provided us with invaluable data.

8. Bibliographical References

Alorainy, W., Burnap, P., Liu, H., and Williams, M. L. (2019). "the enemy among us" detecting cyber hate speech with threats-based othering language embeddings. *ACM Transactions on the Web (TWEB)*, 13(3):1–26.

Badjatiya, P., Gupta, S., Gupta, M., and Varma, V. (2017). Deep learning for hate speech detection in tweets. In *Proceedings of the 26th International Conference on World Wide Web Companion*, pages 759–760. International World Wide Web Conferences Steering Committee.

Bahdanau, D., Cho, K., and Bengio, Y. (2014). Neural machine translation by jointly learning to align and translate. *arXiv preprint arXiv:1409.0473*.

Bojanowski, P., Grave, E., Joulin, A., and Mikolov, T. (2017). Enriching word vectors with subword information. *Transactions of the Association for Computational Linguistics*, 5:135–146.

Burnap, P. and Williams, M. L. (2016a). Us and them: identifying cyber hate on twitter across multiple protected characteristics. *EPJ Data Science*, 5(1):11.

Burnap, P. and Williams, M. L. (2016b). Us and them: identifying cyber hate on twitter across multiple protected characteristics. *EPJ Data Science*, 5(1):11.

Coban, E. B. and Filatova, E. (2019). Incendiary news detection. *Association for the Advancement of Artificial Intelligence*.

Çöltekin, Ç. (2020). A corpus of turkish offensive language on social media. In *Proceedings of the 12th Language Resources and Evaluation Conference*, pages 6174–6184.

De Marneffe, M.-C., MacCartney, B., Manning, C. D., et al. (2006). Generating typed dependency parses from phrase structure parses. In *Lrec*, volume 6, pages 449–454.

Devlin, J., Chang, M.-W., Lee, K., and Toutanova, K. (2019). BERT: Pre-training of deep bidirectional transformers for language understanding. In *Proceedings of the 2019 Conference of the North American Chapter of the Association for Computational Linguistics: Human Language Technologies, Volume 1 (Long and Short Papers)*, pages 4171–4186, Minneapolis, Minnesota, June. Association for Computational Linguistics.

Gitari, N. D., Zuping, Z., Damien, H., and Long, J. (2015). A lexicon-based approach for hate speech detection. *International Journal of Multimedia and Ubiquitous Engineering*, 10(4):215–230.

Hüsünbeyi, Z. M. (2020). Detecting hate speech in turkish texts. Master's thesis, Bogaziçi University.

Jourová, V. (2016). Code of conduct on countering illegal hate speech online: First results on implementation. *European Commission.[cit. 8. březen 2018]*.

Kim, Y. (2014). Convolutional neural networks for sentence classification. In *Proceedings of the 2014 Conference on Empirical Methods in Natural Language Processing (EMNLP)*, pages 1746–1751. Association for Computational Linguistics.

Kress, G. and Hodge, R. (1997). Language as ideology. *The Modern Language Journal*, 64:512.

Le, Q. and Mikolov, T. (2014). Distributed representations of sentences and documents. In *International conference on machine learning*, pages 1188–1196.

Liu, P., Li, W., and Zou, L. (2019). NULI at SemEval-2019 task 6: Transfer learning for offensive language detection using bidirectional transformers. In *Proceedings of the 13th International Workshop on Semantic Evaluation*, pages 87–91, Minneapolis, Minnesota, USA, June. Association for Computational Linguistics.

Mishra, P., Yannakoudakis, H., and Shutova, E. (2019). Tackling online abuse: A survey of automated abuse detection methods. *arXiv preprint arXiv:1908.06024*.

Mishraa, A. K., Saumyab, S., and Kumara, A. (2020). Iiit_dwd@ hasoc 2020: Identifying offensive content in indo-european languages.

Nobata, C., Tetreault, J., Thomas, A., Mehdad, Y., and Chang, Y. (2016). Abusive language detection in online user content. In *Proceedings of the 25th international conference on world wide web*, pages 145–153. International World Wide Web Conferences Steering Committee.

Oktar, L. and Değer, A. C. (1999). Gazete söyleminde kiplik ve İşlevleri. *Dilbilim Araştırmaları Dergisi*, pages 45–53.

Oktar, L. (2001). The ideological organization of representational processes in the presentation of us and them. *Discourse & Society*, 12(3):313–346.

Ozdemir, A. and Yeniterzi, R. (2020). Su-nlp at semeval-2020 task 12: Offensive language identification in turkish tweets. In *Proceedings of the Fourteenth Workshop on Semantic Evaluation*, pages 2171–2176.

Park, J. H. and Fung, P. (2017). One-step and two-step classification for abusive language detection on Twitter. In *Proceedings of the First Workshop on Abusive Language Online*, pages 41–45. Association for Computational Linguistics.

Rogers, A., Kovaleva, O., and Rumshisky, A. (2020). A primer in bertology: What we know about how bert works. *Transactions of the Association for Computational Linguistics*, 8:842–866.

Straka, M. and Straková, J. (2017). Tokenizing, pos tagging, lemmatizing and parsing ud 2.0 with udpipe. In *Proceedings of the CoNLL 2017 Shared Task: Multilingual Parsing from Raw Text to Universal Dependencies*, pages 88–99.

Sulubacak, U., Gokirmak, M., Tyers, F., Çöltekin, Ç., Nivre, J., and Eryiğit, G. (2016). Universal dependencies for turkish. In *Proceedings of COLING 2016, the 26th International Conference on Computational Linguistics: Technical Papers*, pages 3444–3454.

Van Dijk, T. A., (2011). *Discourse, knowledge, power and politics*, pages 27–64.

Wang, S., Liu, J., Ouyang, X., and Sun, Y. (2020). Galileo at semeval-2020 task 12: Multi-lingual learning for offensive language identification using pre-trained language models. In *Proceedings of the Fourteenth Workshop on Semantic Evaluation*, pages 1448–1455.

Wang, C. (2018). Interpreting neural network hate speech classifiers. In *Proceedings of the 2nd Workshop on Abusive Language Online (ALW2)*, pages 86–92.

Waseem, Z. and Hovy, D. (2016). Hateful symbols or hateful people? predictive features for hate speech detection on twitter. In *Proceedings of the NAACL student research workshop*, pages 88–93.

Wiedemann, G., Yimam, S. M., and Biemann, C. (2020). UHH-LT at SemEval-2020 task 12: Fine-tuning of pre-trained transformer networks for offensive language detection. In *Proceedings of the Fourteenth Workshop on Semantic Evaluation*, pages 1638–1644, Barcelona (online), December. International Committee for Computational Linguistics.

Xu, J. M., Jun, K., Zhu, X., and Bellymore, A. (2012). Learning from bullying traces in social media. *Association for Computational Linguistics.*, pages 656–666.

Yang, Z., Yang, D., Dyer, C., He, X., Smola, A., and Hovy, E. (2016). Hierarchical attention networks for document classification. In *Proceedings of the 2016 Conference of the North American Chapter of the Association for Computational Linguistics: Human Language Technologies*, pages 1480–1489, San Diego, California, June. Association for Computational Linguistics.

Yeh, A. (2000). More accurate tests for the statistical significance of result differences. In *COLING 2000 Volume 2: The 18th International Conference on Computational Linguistics*.

Zhang, Z., Robinson, D., and Tepper, J. (2018). Detecting hate speech on twitter using a convolution-gru based deep neural network. In *European Semantic Web Conference*, pages 745–760. Springer.

Çınar, M. (2013). Habercilik ve nefret söylemi. In *Medya ve Nefret Söylemi: Kavramlar, Mecralar, Tartışmalar. Ed. Mahmut ÇINAR.*, İstanbul. Hrant Dink Vakfi Yayınları.

9. Language Resource References

Hrant Dink Foundation. (2021). *The Hate Speech Digital Archive*. Media Watch on Hate Speech project.

Appendix: Reported Speech Forms List

dedi	's/he said'
söyledi	's/he told'
açıkladı	's/he explained/ announced'
açıklar	's/he/it explains/ announces'
açıkladılar	's/he/it explained/ announced'
belirtir	's/he states that'
belirtti	's/he stated that'
belirttiler	'they stated that'
diye konuştu	's/he stated that'
diye konuştular	'they stated that'
kaydetti	's/he noted'
kaydettiler	'they noted'
dile getirdi	's/he mentioned'
dile getirir	's/he mentions'
dile getirdiler	'they mentioned'
uyardı	's/he warned'
uyardılar	'they warned'
uyarır	's/he/it warns'
işaret etti	's/he/it pointed out'
işaret eder	's/he/it points out'
suçladı	's/he blamed/ accused'
suçlar	's/he/it blames/ accuses'
suçladılar	'they blamed/ accused'
tepkilere yol açtı	'it caused reactions'
tepkilere yol açtılar	'they caused reactions'
şikayet etti	's/he reported/ complained'
şikayet eder	's/he reports/ complains'
şikayet ettiler	'they reported/ complained'
karşılık verdi	's/he responded'
karşılık verdiler	'they responded'

Table 3: The list with 30 tokens in Turkish and their English translations to detect news articles including reported speech forms

Proceedings of LATERAISSE Workshop @LREC2022, pages 42–50
Marseille, 25 June 2022
© European Language Resources Association (ELRA), licensed under CC-BY-NC-4.0

An Open Source Contractual Language Understanding Application Using Machine Learning

Afra Nawar*, **Mohammed Rakib***, **Salma Abdul Hai***, **Sanaulla Haq***
North South University
Dhaka-1229, Bangladesh
{afra.nawar05, mohammed.rakib, salma.hai,sanaulla.haq}@northsouth.edu

Abstract

Legal field is characterized by its exclusivity and non-transparency. Despite the frequency and relevance of legal dealings, legal documents like contracts remains elusive to non-legal professionals for the copious usage of legal jargon. There has been little advancement in making legal contracts more comprehensible. This paper presents how Machine Learning (ML) and Natural Language Processing (NLP) can be applied to solve this problem, further considering the challenges of applying ML to the high length of contract documents and training in a low resource environment. The largest open-source contract dataset so far, the Contract Understanding Atticus Dataset (CUAD) is utilized. Various pre-processing experiments and hyperparameter tuning have been carried out and we successfully managed to eclipse SOTA results presented for models in the CUAD dataset trained on RoBERTa-base. Our model, A-type-RoBERTa-base achieved an AUPR score of 46.6% compared to 42.6% on the original RoBERT-base. This model is utilized in our end to end contract understanding application which is able to take a contract and highlight the clauses a user is looking to find along with it's descriptions to aid due diligence before signing. Alongside digital, i.e. searchable, contracts the system is capable of processing scanned, i.e. non-searchable, contracts using tesseract OCR. This application is aimed to not only make contract review a comprehensible process to non-legal professionals, but also to help lawyers and attorneys more efficiently review contracts.

Keywords: Contract Review, Machine Learning, CUAD

1. Introduction

As transactions and interpersonal or business relationships are legalized to an extent greater than ever in precedence, contracts have become one of the most widely utilized legal documents today, enabling legal repercussions, and thus, informed agreement is critical. For legal professionals, who work with numerous clients and documents, the contract review process is a routine and time-consuming task making it is easy to overlook crucial information. For individuals without legal knowledge and unable to attain legal services, the process is esoteric.

Despite the advances of machine learning (ML) and natural language processing (NLP), applied technology in the legal industry which addresses these issues are scarce. Majority of the legal documents, such as judgment papers and contracts are in text format, some even hundreds of pages in length, and difficult to review quickly and accurately. (Hegel et al., 2021). Legal AI is important in the legal industry because it helps save time and effort by reducing the amount of work lawyers have to perform (Dabass and Dabass, 2018). In this paper we apply Machine Learning to contract agreements in order to simplify contract understanding process for the average person and attorneys. As shown in Fig 1, our application allows users to input a contract, and the model provides a labelled contract with the types of clauses recognized, assisting users in making educated legal decisions in a matter of minutes.

*All authors contributed equally to this work

2. Literature Review

Legal judgment prediction, legal entity recognition, document classification, legal question answering, and legal summarization are some of the tasks which have been explored using Machine learning and NLP. Legal Artificial Intelligence (LegalAI) is a branch of artificial intelligence that focuses on assisting lawyers with legal duties.

Authors in (Zhong et al., 2020) demonstrate numerous embedding- and symbol-based approaches and discuss LegalAI's future path. They have gone through three common applications in detail, including judgment prediction, similar case matching, and legal question answering, to show why these two types of techniques are critical to LegalAI. Malik et al. (Malik et al., 2021) introduce the INDIAN LEGAL DOCUMENTS CORPUS (ILDC), a collection of Supreme Court of India case processes (SCI). Their best prediction model presents a 78% accuracy compared to 94% for human legal experts.

In another study (Holzenberger et al., 2020), the authors present the Statutory Reasoning Assessment dataset (SARA), which consists of a collection of rules taken from the US Internal Revenue Code (IRC) laws, as well as a set of natural language questions that can only be answered properly by referring to the rules. They have offered a legal statutes resource, a collection of hand-curated natural language rules and cases, and a symbolic solver capable of representing these rules and solving the challenge task. This study is intended to be a contribution to legal-domain natural language processing, in addition to the fascinating challenge provided by statutory reasoning.

In (Roegiest et al., 2018) the authors propose different models for the due diligence problem to find specific clauses in legal contractual documents and quantify the risk associated with each. They also introduce a new dataset, a subset of their production dataset, with 15 million sentences in 4200 contracts. This goal is quite similar to ours, however they did not approach the problem with Deep Learning, rather with linear classifiers, Conditional Random Fields (CRF), hybrid models of SVM and Hidden Markov Models. The best and most reliable result was achieved through CRF.

In (Hendrycks et al., 2021) they've compiled a high-quality dataset of annotated contracts to aid contract analysis research and to learn more about how well NLP models work in highly specialized domains. Over 13,000 annotations by legal experts are included in CUAD through 41 labels. On CUAD, we tested ten pretrained language models and discovered that their performance is promising, but there is still much space for improvement. They have also discovered that data is a major bottleneck, as reducing data by an order of magnitude drastically reduces efficiency, emphasizing the importance of CUAD's large number of annotations. They also discovered that model design has a significant impact on efficiency, implying that algorithmic advances from the NLP group would aid in resolving this issue. They concluded that the CUAD has the potential to speed up research into a major real-world issue while also acting as a benchmark for evaluating NLP models on specialized domains in general. The authors in (Leivaditi et al., 2020) provide another dataset for contract review, however, with fewer categories and annotations than CUAD.

One recent work done in this field, (Hegel et al., 2021), shows that the visual cues like layout, style, and placement of text in a document are significant elements that are important to obtaining an acceptable degree of accuracy on long documents.

3. METHODOLOGY

The system diagram, delineating the work flow of our application, is shown in Fig-1. The dataset is first split into three parts: training, validation and testing. Next, the text of each of the parts is converted to tokens and then the tokens are embedded to tensors. After this, the dataset is trained using pretrained transformer models and then evaluated. Subsequently, the best performing model is selected and quantized in order to deploy the model with the backend. Finally, the user can do inference on any legal contract. Each of the blocks below will be briefly explained in this section, along with their significance.

3.1. CUAD Dataset

We are using Contract Understanding Atticus Dataset (CUAD) for training and evaluating our model. It contains 510 contracts with 13101 labeled clauses. There are 25 different types of contracts with varying lengths ranging from a few pages to over one hundred pages. But, most parts of a contract should not be highlighted. Labeled clauses make up about 10% of each contract on average. Since there are 41 label categories, this means that on average, only about 0.25% of each contract is highlighted for each label. We have divided the dataset into two parts — 80% for training and 20% for testing. In terms of feeding the data to our model, there are 22450 training samples and 4182 test samples. Each sample has four keys: 'id', 'title', 'context', 'question', 'answers'. The 'answers' key has two parts: the answer itself as text and the starting index of the answer in the context. Our model will predict the starting index and text of the answer after completion of its training.

3.2. Tokenizing Inputs and Embedding Tokens

Before feeding the texts of our document to any model, we need to preprocess them. This is done by the Transformer Tokenizer (Wolf et al., 2019). Each model has its own tokenizer, which converts input text to tokens, including converting the tokens to their corresponding IDs in the vocabulary and put it in a format the model expects, as well as generate the other inputs that the model requires. Since we will be using pre-trained models, we will utilize the vocabulary and tokenizer used while pre-training these models. The next step in the workflow is to breathe meaning to the tokens so that the model can understand the relationship among the tokens and make sense out of them. This is done by converting each token into a vector representation of numbers called a tensor. But before embedding the tokens into tensors, the tokens for very long documents are handled by truncating the context to the max length that our model can fit. Moreover, in order to account for the case in which the answer lies at the point we split a long context, we allow some overlap between the features.

3.3. Training and Evaluating Pretrained Transformer Models

Pretrained models are models that have already undergone extensive training on massive datasets, which are then applied to downstream tasks through fine-tuning. We are using pre-trained transformer models since these significantly improve results, compared to training from scratch, for many NLP tasks like Question Answering, Machine Translation, Named Entity Recognition, etc. We aim to fine-tune pre-trained transformer models by retraining them for Question Answering Task since our CUAD dataset is based on it. Besides, we perform various experiments by trying different combinations of hyperparameters to evaluate and improve the performance of these models, which are broadly explained in the experiment and results section.

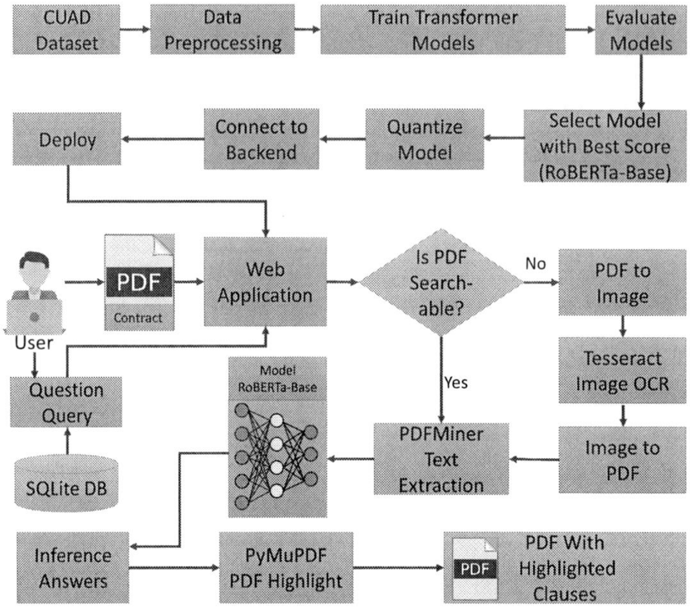

Figure 1: System Diagram of Our Project.

3.4. Quantization

Quantization refers to a method of computing and storing tensors with smaller bitwidths instead of floating point precision to enable deep learning models to run quicker and use less memory. There are 3 types of quantization: 1) Dynamic Quantization 2) Static Quantization 3) Quantization-Aware Training. We implemented dynamic quantization which quantizes the weights beforehand whereas the activations are quantized at runtime (Peng et al., 2007). We have used Dynamic quantization as it is the most simple one of the three and can be applied on-the-fly without requiring to retrain the model.

3.5. Application

3.5.1. Backend

In order to make the trained model useful in the real world an end to end system was implemented wherein users may upload their contracts and perform clause-wise inference on the contracts to allow them to easily and quickly evaluate the contract and perform due diligence.

The web application returns inferences from our trained model underneath the user interface. The user may upload their contract and select out of the 41 clauses they wish to quickly identify, starting the backend inference process. When the user uploads their PDF it goes straight to our text extraction module with PDFMiner Library. It extracts text from PDF documents with 97% accuracy calculated using Levenshtein Distance compared to the extracted texts in the test set of original CUAD dataset. If, however, the PDFS are scanned, i.e. non searchable, they are passed to OCR PDF conversion function to generate a searchable PDF. This PDF is passed to the PDFMiner module like before, the consequent processes being identical.

The extracted text is passed as the context along with the selected clause or question query to the trained Roberta-Base model as features. It performs the inference and returns it to our Highlighting module which calculates the rectangular positions of the answers within the user's PDF and draws highlights around it. The app is reloaded to show the user the answer.[1]

3.5.2. Searchable PDF Conversion

In order for the model to deliver an inference, the extracted texts from the input contract must be fed into it. To extract the contract's contents, we utilized PDFminer. However, this approach only works with native/searchable PDF files, not scanned/non-searchable ones. We tested Tesseract (Tesseract-Ocr,) and EasyOCR (JaidedAI,) and compared their accuracy to guarantee that the texts are accurat5ely retrieved from scanned files. For Tesseract to perform well, it is essential that the quality of the images are enhanced before it is input into the OCR. To provide a general solution, image preprocessing techniques were used to eliminate any distorted or potentially poor images. As shown in the Fig-2 below, converting the image to grayscale, binarization, noise removal using di-

[1]The web application and model are available at github.com/afra-tech/defactolaw

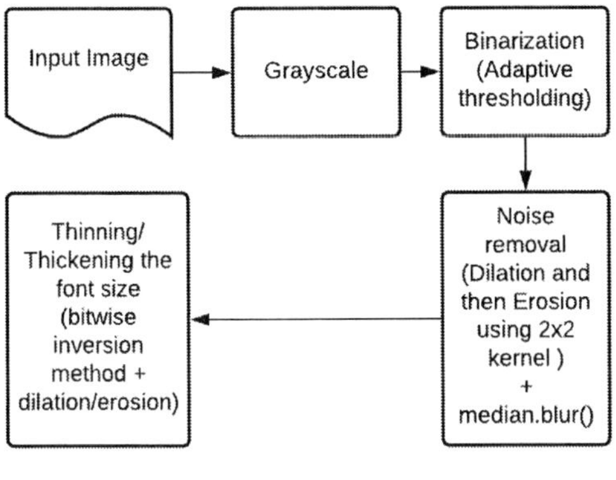

Figure 2: Flowchart of Image Preprocessing.

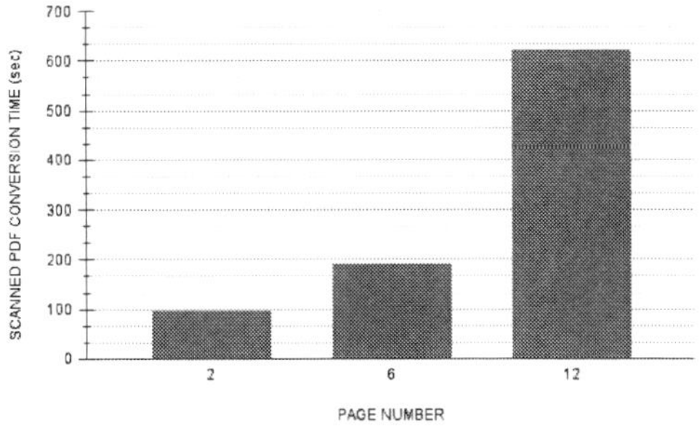

Figure 3: Scanned to Searchable PDF Conversion Time.

lation and erosion, median blur, and thinning or thickening the fonts using dilation, erosion, and bitwise invert methods were all part of the preprocessing.

The adaptive threshold was chosen for the experiment because it is considerably better for situations involving text extraction. The block size, which is one of the parameters in adaptive threshold, determines the size of the neighbourhood area and C is a constant that is subtracted from the mean or weighted sum of the neighbourhood pixels. To determine these two parameters has been a challenge. Since, low noise (Higher value of C) resulted in fainted texts and higher noise (Low value of C) resulted in illegible images. Because only certain noise is required for proper text readability, it was necessary to eliminate it using morphological operations such as dilation and erosion. In order to remove pixels that do not correspond to text that are still surrounding text items or perhaps the noise, the binarized images were first dilated and then eroded. In the dilation, A 2x2 kernel or matrix was created, and the entire image was convolutioned. Dilation increases the amount of whitespace in the image, which reduces noise and tiny dark areas. Erosion works in a similar way, except it increases the darkness of the letters and makes them easier to read. For erosion, the same kernel size was utilized. The image was slightly blurred after the two processes and the overall salt and pepper noise in the image was eliminated as a result of this. For thinning/thickening the font, the image was initially inverted to make dilation and erosion make sense. The background is now black, but the text is white. Now, erosion with a kernel size of 2x2 was employed to make the typefaces narrower. The same technique was used to thicken the font size, only the erosion process was substituted with dilation with the same kernel size.

However, the extracted texts' accuracy was not sufficient (less than 50%). Various issues in the input data, such as different layouts, skewness, and typefaces, hindered successful recognition. In comparison to Tesseract, EasyOCR did slightly better at extracting texts. Using EasyOCR speeds up the process since Tesseract requires pre-processing of non-scanned images to make them seem like scanned images in order to function well, which increases the overall inference time. However, the accuracy of the retrieved texts can not always be guaranteed. The overall application time is increased since extracting texts from scanned PDF takes time and converting the scanned PDF to a searchable PDF for highlighting the text clauses also takes some time. As a result, a general approach was offered, which is described below.

We have tested the use of tesseract output HOCR. HOCR is an open data representation standard for structured text generated by optical character recognition (OCR). Because the text, style, layout information, recognition confidence metrics, and other data are encoded using Extensible Markup Language (XML) in the form of Hypertext Markup Language (HTML) or XHTML (Breuel, 2007), this worked perfectly for our system. The scanned PDF is converted to searchable PDF using tesseract output in HOCR and storing the result as PDF. This is now used for text extraction by applying the corresponding implementation of extracting texts from searchable PDF as discussed before. The retrieved texts using this technique have an accuracy that ranges from 93.99% to 99.09%. Fig-3 illustrates the time it takes to convert a scanned PDF to searchable PDF vs. the amount of pages it contains. As it can be observed, the time grows exponentially as the PDF's content increases. This is due to the internal process of converting the PDF to images, and subsequently from images to HOCR and lastly to a searchable PDF.

4. Experiments and Results

4.1. Transformer Models

4.1.1. Evaluation Metric

We have used four evaluation metrics which are: Exact Match, F1 Score, Area under Precision Recall Curve (AUPR) and Precision @80% Recall. In the dataset's paper (Hendrycks et al., 2021), Precision @90% Recall is only non-zero for DeBERTa x-large, which we have not trained due to insufficient resources, hence the metric is not evaluated.

1. **Exact Match:** This metric is as simple as it sounds. For each question-answer pair, EM=1 if the characters of the model's prediction exactly match the characters of the True Answer, otherwise EM=0.

2. **F1 Score:** F1 score is a typical metric for classification problems and is generally utilized in QA. The number of shared words between the prediction and the truth is the basis of the F1 score: precision is the ratio of the number of shared words to the total number of words in the prediction, and recall is the ratio of the number of shared words to the total number of words in the ground truth. We will be evaluating F1 Scores of questions that have answers since this tells us how accurately our model could highlight the desired labels in the contract. F 1 Score $=2 \times \frac{Precision \times Recall}{Precision + Recall}$

3. **Area Under Precision Recall Curve (AUPR):** A precision-recall curve shows the relationship between precision (= positive predictive value) and recall (= sensitivity) for every possible selected cut-off. The area under this curve is called AUPR. It represents the average precision of a model. The more the area the better the model. AUPR is suitable for imbalanced datasets as this metric is not affected by a large no. of negative or positive examples compared to their counterparts.

4. **Precision at 80% Recall:** As our main goal is to review legal contracts, it is of huge importance that our model does not misclassify any positive labels (important parts which are required to be highlighted). For this reason, a high recall (no. of positives predicted correctly out of all the actual positives in the dataset) is necessary and so we fix our recall at 80% threshold and then measure precision which is a good indicator of how well our model can review contracts.

4.1.2. Major Contributions in Improving Performance of Models

1. **Training Large No. of Models:** We have trained a total of 75 models of different types using various hyperparameters to find out the best model. Fig-4 shows the performance (Exact-Match Score) of all the 75 models trained during this process. Observing the figure we see that there are a lot of models with very good, very bad as well as average performances. So we set a baseline score of 60% shown by the red line in Fig-4. So, in this paper we will broadly explain only the models that have an Exact Match score of 60% or more.

2. **Balancing Features:** A contract, on average, has 10% of labeled clauses. So, after converting to features, more than 99% of them do not contain any of the 41 relevant labels. To mitigate this imbalance, we drop a significant portion of the features that do not contain any relevant labels so that features are approximately balanced between having highlighted clauses and not having any highlighted clauses. As a result, we see a significant improvement in training times and performance gains as there is a balance between highlighted and unhighlighted parts. To be more specific, observing Fig-5 we can see that training time was reduced by 48 times and performance of models also increased by 1.5 times. So balancing features played a crucial role in training the models in a resource-efficient manner as well as improving performance scores.

4.1.3. Optimal Hyper-parameters

The optimal hyperparameters for all our experiments are shown in Table-1. We have tried numerous combinations of various hyperparameters as shown in Table-2 and observed that the hyper-parameter values in Table-1 give the best results. It is important to note that all the optimal values are based on a single GPU with 12GB or 16GB VRAM. Besides, all our experiments were conducted in a resource constrained environment.

Table 1: Optimal Hyperparameters

Hyperparameter	Default Value
Learning Rate	3x10-5
Batch Size	16
Epochs	4
Weight Decay	0.01
Gradient Accumulation Step	2
Eval Accumulation Steps	1
Max Length	384
Doc Stride	128

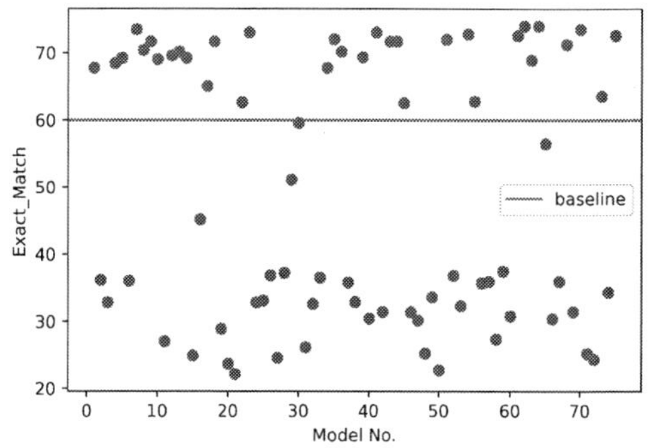

Figure 4: Scatter plot of Exact Match Performances of All Models Trained

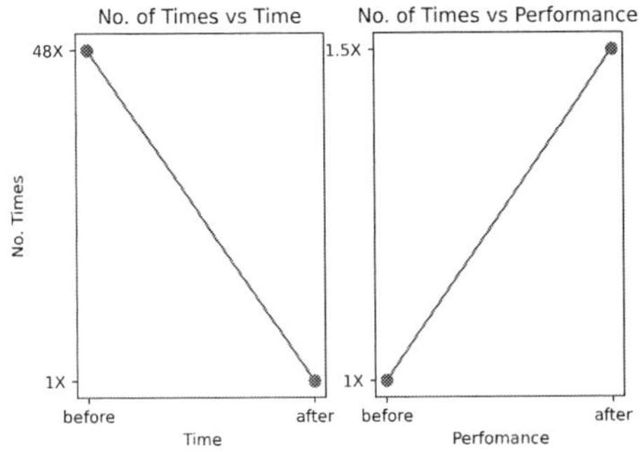

Figure 5: Before-After Plot of Performance and Training Time for Balancing Features.

Table 2: Range of Hyperparameters Tested to Find Optimal Hyperparameters

Hyperparameter	Range of Values
Learning Rate	1x10-4, 3x10-4, 3x10-3, 3x10-5, 3x10-7
Batch Size	2, 4, 8, 16, 24
Epochs	2, 4, 8
Weight Decay	0.01
Gradient Accumulation Step	1, 2, 4, 8, 16, 20
Eval Accumulation Steps	1, 2, 4, 8, 16, 20
Max Length	256, 384, 512
Doc Stride	128, 256

4.1.4. Original Models

Original models are the ones provided by the owners of the CUAD dataset. They have performed grid search to find out optimum parameters and then trained these models on their dataset. Table-3 shows the performance of these models and Table-4 shows the optimum hyperparameters. They have used multiple GPUs in parallel for achieving such results with no limit on computational power.

Table 3: Original CUAD Models

Model Name	AUPR	Precision at 80% Recall	Exact Match	F1 Score
albert-xlarge	37.8	20.5	-	-
roberta-base	42.6	31.1	73.5	81.8
roberta-large	48.2	38.1	74.0	84.8

4.1.5. RoBERTa

We have selected RoBERTa (Liu et al., 2019) since it is an improved version of BERT and the base version has suitable parameters for our computationally restricted environment. The RoBERTa models performed best on both AUPR scores and Exact Match scores. Since we will be reviewing contracts, the AUPR score and Precision at 80% recall is quite important. Comparing RoBERTa with other models like Longformer and ALBERT in Fig-6 we see that no other transformer type comes close to RoBERTa in terms of AUPR. Observing Table-3 and Table-5, we can see that, the B-type-roberta-base (AUPR-46.8) has eclipsed the AUPR score of the original SOTA RoBERTa base (AUPR-42.6) by a healthy margin of 4.2% which is commendable. This was possible due to the proper tuning and optimal selection of hyperparameters from various combinations. The original SOTA score for precision at 80% recall is 31.1% for RoBERTa-base and we have managed to get a score of 29.6% which is also quite good. If we compare these scores to the original SOTA RoBERTa-large, we see that the RoBERTa-large has an AUPR of 48.2% which is 1.4% higher than our RoBERTa base. But if we check the Precision at 80% Recall scores then our best RoBERTa-base model is behind by a lot. The RoBERTa-large model has a Precision at 80% Recall score of 38.1% whereas our best model has a score of 29.6%. Now, if we come to the Exact Match scores, we see that the SOTA RoBERTa-base model has an exact match score of 73.5% whereas our best model (roberta-base-squad2) has an exact match score of 74% which is a minor improvement. Now, in order to get these results, we had to specifically tune the model to get best results at that particular metric. This resulted in multiple models each giving high scores at a particular metric. For example: best AUPR score of 46.8% was given by B-type-roberta-base model, best Exact Match score of 74% was given by roberta-base-squad2 model and best Precision at 80% Recall of 29.6% was given by A-type-roberta-base model. However, if we were to select a model which gives decent scores in all of the criteria then roberta-base-squad2-nq model should be selected. This model has an AUPR score of 43.4%, Precision at 80% Recall score of 28.1% and Exact Match score of 70.12%

4.1.6. ALBERT

We tried our dataset on Albert (Lan et al., 2020) since it has a good record in question-answering tasks and performs pretty well in the SQUAD-v2 dataset outperforming BERT. But unfortunately, we see that the results are not quite satisfactory. We have tried various ALBERT models and the best performing one among them is ALBERT-xlarge-v2. It has an AUPR of 37.5%, Precision at 80% Recall of 25.2% and Exact Match of 72% as shown in Table-5. Out of all, only the Exact Match score is close to the SOTA model. The rest are quite far off. So, we stopped further pursuing this model due to poor performance and resource constraints.

Table 4: Hyperparameters of Models Used in Experiments

Hyperparameter / Model	Learning Rate	Batch Size	Epochs	Decay	Gradient Accumulation Step	Eval Accumulation Steps	Max Length	Doc Stride
DistilRoBERTa-base	3x10-5	4	4	0.1	8	8	384	128
Longformer-base-squad2								
ALBERT-xlarge-v2								
RoBERTa-base-squad2								
RoBERTa-base-squad2-nq								
A-typeRoBERTa-base-squad2-nq	3x10-5	16	4	0.1	2	1	384	128
A-type-RoBERTa-base								
B-type-RoBERTa-base	3x10-5	24	4	0.1	1	1	384	128

Table 5: Performance of All Models

Model Names	AUPR	Precision @ 80% Recall	Exact_Match	F1 Score
DistilRoBERTa-base	35.9	18.6	67.8	79
Longformer-base-squad2	36.4	21.3	73.1	84.3
ALBERT-xlarge-v2	37.5	25.2	72	83.6
RoBERTa-base-squad2	41.4	22.3	74	84.5
A-type-RoBERTa-base-squad2-nq	42.7	27.3	72.7	83
RoBERTa-base-squad2-nq	43.4	28.1	70.12	80.9
A-type-RoBERTa-base	46.6	29.6	65	74.4
B-type-RoBERTa-base	46.8	25	59.6	68.2

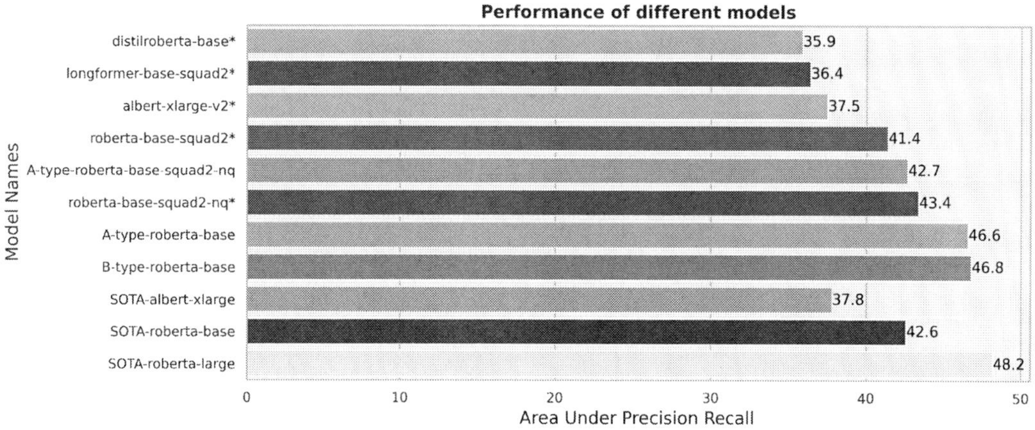

Figure 6: Comparison of AUPR Scores of All Models

4.1.7. Longformer

Longformer (Beltagy et al., 2020) is the extended version of the RoBERTa specifically trained on long documents from where the checkpoint of the RoBERTa model ends. Since legal documents can be very long and our dataset has documents that consist of more than 100 pages, we decided to use the Longformer model. The results from the Longformer model is also not upto the mark. We experimented with various longformer models and are reporting only the best one among them. The best longformer with our default hyperparameters is longformer-base that has been fine tuned on squad-v2 and then trained on our dataset. It has an AUPR score of 36.4%, Precision at 80% Recall of 21.3% and Exact Match score of 73.1% as shown in Table-5. This model has a noteworthy Exact Match score since it is only 0.4% behind the original RoBERTa base model. The results of the other metrics are very poor.

4.2. Distil-RoBERTa-base

Knowledge distillation is the process of transferring knowledge from a large model to a smaller model without loss of validity. Distil-RoBERTa-base is a model where the knowledge of RoBERTa-base was trans-

Table 6: Quantization Results

Roberta Base	Exact Match	F1 Score	Size
Before Quantization	65	74.4	500MB
After Quantization	41.4	44.7	240MB

ferred to it while reducing the number of trainable parameters and size. So, for our case the model size was reduced by about 160MB and parameters decreased by 28M compared to the regular RoBERTa-base model. The performance of this model with respect to its reduced size and parameters is good but not sufficient enough. It has an AUPR score of 35.9%, Precision at 80% Recall of 18.6% and Exact Match score of 67.8% as shown in Table-5.

4.2.1. Comparison Among All Models

Since the main purpose of these models is to review contracts, a high recall is a must. We don't want the model to misclassify any positive labels (important parts which are required to be highlighted). For this reason, a high recall (no. of positives predicted correctly out of all the actual positives in the dataset) is necessary along with high precision (no. of positives predicted correctly out of all the positives predicted by the model). For this reason, the models with high Precision@ 80% Recall and high AUPR (average precision of the model) should be selected. Analyzing Fig-6 and Table-5, we can come to a conclusion that for our task, A-type-RoBERTa-base is the best model as it has the highest Precision @80% Recall of 29.6% and second-highest AUPR score of 46.6% (highest 46.8%). Although A-type-RoBERTa-base has the highest AUPR score of 46.8% it falls significantly behind in the Precision @80% Recall metric with a score of 25%. So, we decided to use the A-type-RoBERTa base model for our project.

4.2.2. Quantized Model Performance

To reduce the model size for more space conscious deployment, we applied quantization on our best model, A-type-RoBERTa-base model. This allowed reduction of the model size from 500mb to 240mb which is a 50% decrease in size just by quantizing the linear layers. However, while evaluating the results are not quite up to the mark. The results in Table-6 are for dynamic quantization which quantizes the weights beforehand whereas the activations are quantized at runtime. So we see that, the exact match score decreases by 36% and the F1 Score decreases by 39%.

5. Conclusion

In this paper, we present a machine learning and NLP powered application for automatic contract review utilizing the open source CUAD question answering dataset. We presented the logical workflow of the application along with our trials and experiments and with different tools and technologies for each functional step.

Legal documents are inherently lengthy, and we've outlined the challenges of applying ML and NLP processing to them under resource constraints, due to which we were unable to carry out our experiments utilizing larger transformers, such as DeBERTa-xlarge. Nevertheless, we achieve a higher AUPR score for the RoBERTa base model compared to the results of the CUAD paper (Hendrycks et al., 2021). We also present our experiments into text extraction from contracts which are both searchable, i.e. digitally created or text overlaid documents, and non-searchable i.e. scanned documents to allow users to upload contracts from different sources.

Our application is open source and available on github, as cited in section 3.5.1. With our work we aim to contribute towards open source tools and technologies in the legal field for legal professionals and the general public without legal education and means to afford legal services for professional contract review.

Appendix: Application Overview

Fig-7 portrays the pictorial shots of our front-end.

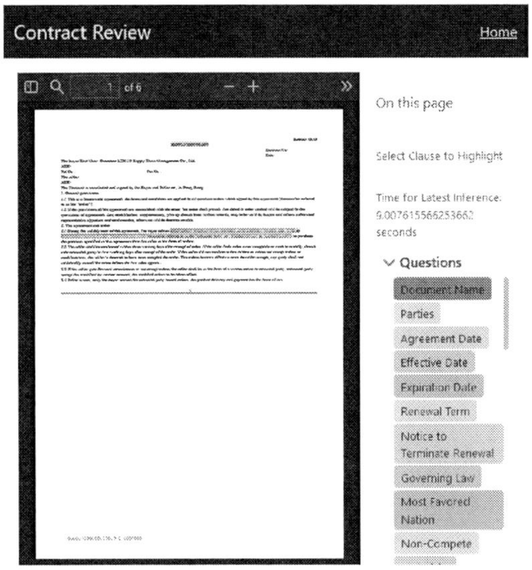

Figure 7: Screenshot of Legal Contract Review Application

6. Bibliographical References

Beltagy, I., Peters, M. E., and Cohan, A. (2020). Longformer: The Long-Document Transformer.

Breuel, T. M. (2007). The hOCR Microformat for OCR Workflow and Results. In *Ninth International Conference on Document Analysis and Recognition (ICDAR 2007)*, volume 2, pages 1063–1067. IEEE.

Dabass, J. and Dabass, B. S. (2018). Scope of Artificial Intelligence in Law.

Hegel, A., Shah, M., Peaslee, G., Roof, B., and Elwany, E. (2021). The Law of Large Documents: Understanding the Structure of Legal Contracts Using Visual Cues. *arXiv preprint arXiv:2107.08128*.

Hendrycks, D., Burns, C., Chen, A., and Ball, S. (2021). CUAD: An Expert-Annotated NLP Dataset for Legal Contract Review. *arXiv preprint arXiv:2103.06268*.

Holzenberger, N., Blair-Stanek, A., and Van Durme, B. (2020). A Dataset for Statutory Reasoning in Tax Law Entailment and Question Answering. *arXiv preprint arXiv:2005.05257*.

JaidedAI.). JaidedAI/EasyOCR: Ready-to-use OCR with 80 Supported Languages and All popular Writing Scripts.

Lan, Z., Chen, M., Goodman, S., Gimpel, K., Sharma, P., and Soricut, R. (2020). ALBERT: A Lite BERT for Self-supervised Learning of Language Representations.

Leivaditi, S., Rossi, J., and Kanoulas, E. (2020). A Benchmark for Lease Contract Review. *arXiv preprint arXiv:2010.10386*.

Liu, Y., Ott, M., Goyal, N., Du, J., Joshi, M., Chen, D., Levy, O., Lewis, M., Zettlemoyer, L., and Stoyanov, V. (2019). RoBERTa: A Robustly Optimized BERT Pretraining Approach.

Malik, V., Sanjay, R., Nigam, S. K., Ghosh, K., Guha, S. K., Bhattacharya, A., and Modi, A. (2021). ILDC for CJPE: Indian Legal Documents Corpus for Court Judgment Prediction and Explanation. *arXiv preprint arXiv:2105.13562*.

Peng, H., Prodic, A., Alarcón, E., and Maksimovic, D. (2007). Modeling of Quantization Effects in Digitally Controlled dc–dc Converters. *IEEE Transactions on power electronics*, 22(1):208–215.

Roegiest, A., Hudek, A. K., and McNulty, A. (2018). A Dataset and an Examination of Identifying Passages for Due Diligence. In *The 41st International ACM SIGIR Conference on Research & Development in Information Retrieval*, pages 465–474.

Tesseract-Ocr.). tesseract-ocr/tesseract: Tesseract Open Source OCR Engine (main repository).

Wolf, T., Debut, L., Sanh, V., Chaumond, J., Delangue, C., Moi, A., Cistac, P., Rault, T., Louf, R., Funtowicz, M., and Brew, J. (2019). HuggingFace's Transformers: State-of-the-art Natural Language Processing. *CoRR*, abs/1910.03771.

Zhong, H., Xiao, C., Tu, C., Zhang, T., Liu, Z., and Sun, M. (2020). How does NLP Benefit Legal System: A Summary of Legal Artificial Intelligence. *arXiv preprint arXiv:2004.12158*.

Author Index